DANCE FROM HEAVEN TO EARTH

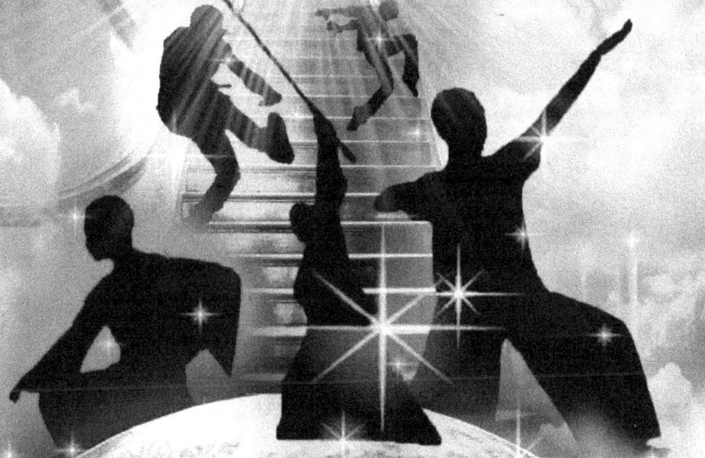

TAQUETTA BAKER & NINA COOK

Book Synopsis: *"Dance From Heaven to Earth!" is a teaching manual purposed to build dance ministers who desire to embody a greater dimension of revelation, knowledge, word, consecration, and spiritual fortitude within their ministry of dance. This book is designed to produce next level dancers who understand the profoundness of their spiritual identity and the depths of ministerial power God has given them in their ministry of dance. Through the impartation of this book, your personal dance ministry and dance teams will be shifted in how you approach ministry, pray about your ministry, prepare for ministry, cultivate your ministry, choreograph, dance with intentional destructive power, and equip yourself for events and services. A new dancer who operates as a portal of heaven into the earth will be birthed, as you fill yourself with the revelation in this book and begin to apply it to your life. The knowledge provided will build heaven's dancers and you will bring the kingdom of heaven into the regions, territories, and lives you impact. Dance from heaven to earth! SHIFT!*

(Website) Kingdomshifters.com

(Email) manifoldgrace5@gmail.com

(Email) kingdomshifters@gmail.com

Connect with Nina & Taquetta via Email, Facebook or YouTube

Nina's Bio

***Nina Cook** has been saved since childhood and has been active in ministry much of her life. Nina carries an apostolic mantle with giftings in dance, singing, production, all manner of prayer, spiritual warfare, deliverance, healing, teaching, pastoring, scribing, and wellness. Nina graduated from Ball State University in 2014 with a Bachelor's Degree. She studied Exercise Science and minored in Dance. Nina has over five years of experience in the wellness and exercise field and 11 years and counting of dance experience.*

Nina is an Elder at Kingdom Shifters Christian Empowerment Center in Muncie, Indiana. She is the main armor bearer for her pastor and is also training in her calling as an apostle. Nina is the founder of "Manifold Grace Production Company" and "Exercise to Life." It is her vision that her production company brings transformation to people and regions through the power and creativity of the arts. Nina is an extraordinary teacher and minister of movement, choreography, atmospheric worship, and using dance and movement in warfare and intercession. Nina provides fitness coaching and exercise and dance class through "Exercise to Life." She utilizes a vast variety of exercise and fitness styles that people can do that are combined with scriptural focuses, short teachings, prayers, and declarations and decrees such that when people do the exercises their bodies are transformed. It is her vision to see people transformed through bringing healing and deliverance to the physical body in areas that hinder their health and wellness, and to also see complete lifestyle changes that shift people into wholeness.

Nina is dedicated to living her life sold out to Christ. She is generally the first to volunteer and take risks for anything that grows the kingdom. She is always seeking to learn, develop, and cultivate herself in the integrity, character, fruit and will of God.

Connect with Nina and Manifold Grace Production Company and "Exercise to Life" at Manifoldgrace5@gmail.com, kingdomshifters.com or via Facebook, and Youtube.

Taquetta's Bio

***Taquetta Baker** is the founder of Kingdom Shifters Ministries (KSM). She has authored fourteen books and two decree CD's. Taquetta has a Master's Degree in Community Counseling with an emphasis on Marriage, Children and Family Counseling, a Bachelor's Degree in Psychology and Associates Degree in Business Administration. In addition, Taquetta has a Therapon Belief Therapist Certification from Therapon Institute and has over 20 years of professional and Christian Counseling experience.*

Taquetta is also gifted at empowering and assisting people with launching ministries, businesses and books and provides mentoring, counseling and vision casting through Kingdom Shifters Kingdom Wellness Program. Taquetta serves on the Board of Directors for New Day Community Ministries, Inc. of Muncie, IN. In October 2008, Taquetta graduated from the Eagles Dance Institute under Dr. Pamela Hardy and received her license in liturgical dance. Before launching into her own ministry, Taquetta served at her previous church for 12 years. She was a prophet, pioneer and leader of Shekinah Expressions Dance Ministry, teacher, member of the presbytery board, and overseer of the Altar Workers Ministry. Taquetta receives mentoring and ministry covering from Bishop Jackie Green, Founder of JGM-National PrayerLife Institute (Phoenix, AZ), and was ordained as an Apostle on June 7, 2014.

Taquetta flows through the wells of warfare and worship and mantles an apostolic mandate of judging and establishing God's kingdom in people, ministries, communities, and regions. Taquetta travels in foreign missions and throughout the United States. She has mentored and established dance, altar workers, deliverance, and prophetic ministries. Taquetta ministers in the areas of fine arts, all manners of prayer, fivefold ministry, deliverance, healing, miracles, atmospheric worship, and empowers and train people in their destiny and life's vision.

Connect with Taquetta and KSM at kingdomshifters.com or via Facebook. For more information regarding Bishop Jackie Green at Jgmenternational.org.

Table of Contents

Table of Contents Continued

Chapter 1
Defined By God

By: Minister Nina Cook

This chapter is multi-dimensional. It is going to discuss the significance of being personally defined, being defined as a dance minister, and defining your dance ministry.

It is of great significance that we are defined, because once we are defined, we are given identity. To be effective dancers who embody the spiritual depth of bringing heaven to earth, we need to know who we are.

Define in Dictionary.com means:

1. To state or set forth the meaning of (a word, phrase, etc.)
2. To explain or identify the nature or essential qualities of; describe
3. To fix or lay down clearly and definitely; specify distinctly
4. To determine or fix the boundaries or extent of
5. To make clear the outline or form of

Some of the synonyms of define are:
characterize, detail, illustrate, and formalize

As we are defined by God, we are:

1. Given meaning
2. Described, and our nature and qualities are identified
3. Clarified, and distinction comes forth
4. Our fixed functions and boundaries are identified and as we are defined by God our bounds only come from Him
5. Our form is made clear and is outlined, we receive the blueprint of who we are

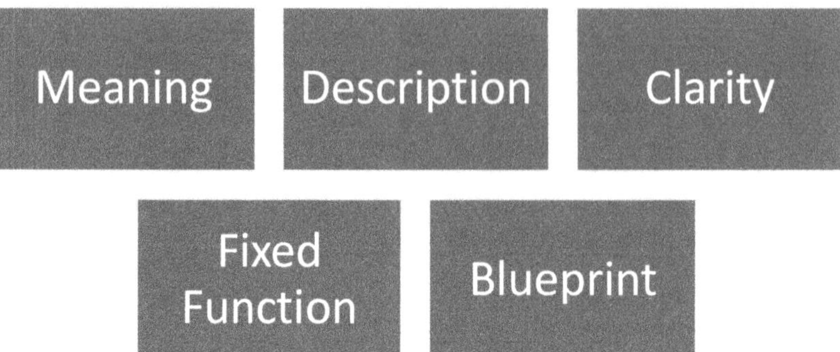

God does the defining before you come into the earth. You are defined in your mother's womb.

> ***Psalms 139:13*** *For you created my inmost being; you knit me together in my mother's womb.*
>
> ***Psalms 139:16*** *Your eyes saw my unformed body; all the days ordained for me were written in your book before one of them came to be.*
>
> ***Ephesians 1:4*** *Even before he made the world, God loved us and chose us in Christ to be holy and without fault in his eyes.*

From these scripture passages above, we see that God is indeed the definer.

- You cannot define yourself
- Interactions and experiences you have endured through life cannot define you
- People cannot define you
- Dance itself and how others view your dance cannot define you

People can walk with you, empower and encourage you, and help you to shift into the definition God has placed in you, but they cannot define you. People come to know who you are by the Spirit of God and not of themselves. They cannot give you anything that God has not already purposed for you, and they cannot just give you what they want, as that is not the truth of who you are. God gives definition and purpose to everything.

> ***Ecclesiastes 3:1*** *For everything there is a season, and a time for every matter under heaven.*

You must know your identity and understand your design because there are many identity ideologies being released today. Each of them has a desire to define you, dictate how you should be, root in your identity, and establish you in falsehood. Seeking God for definition avoids identity pollution such that we can be purebred in God and his original intent for us.

God has a unique intent for who you are as a dancer, and definition helps you understand how you function and why. Once you understand your overall function and distinct purpose, you will have greater perspective, direction, focus, and significance concerning your dance. Having this knowledge of your intentional design will make you more effective as a minister because you can utilize your unique gifts and attributes more frequently and skillfully.

On the contrary, lack of definition:

- Opens the door for confusion and struggle to find yourself. You may look for places to fit in and places to be used which is dangerous if you do not know who you are and what your purpose is.
- You find a place to fit in by circumstance or familiarity which cannot nurture, cultivate, sow into and help you find your authentic self.
- You may waver between different places going through the motions, thus welcoming anything and anyone to define you.

- ❖ You become susceptible to being used, abused be treated as you have no perspective of this within yourself.
- ❖ People can put you where they want and shape you in what is advantageous for them.
- ❖ You may experience times of emptiness where your identity should be, and the enemy may use this as an opening to define you by the abuse you endured. Eventually, many will accept the abuse believing that it is their fault. Once room is given to this thought, you identify with it, expecting to be treated in this manner. Consequently, a pattern forms.
- ❖ The enemy may set out to bring destruction through rejection, abuse, control, misuse, being outcast, used up, and on and on and on, until he annihilates you. He will desire to kill any inkling of passion and love you have for your gifts and ministry shifting you into hating and not acknowledging them. This is a form of self-hatred, which will result in a false identity being taken on.

In this condition of wounded and broken identity, your dance will be halted from flowing in purity and authenticity. As a dancer, whatever challenges present in , and mistreated because you cannot assert how you should you will be released upon the people and regions that receive of you. The confusion, mixture, rejection, hurt, and abuse will be enmeshed into your dance making your ministry perverted and of little to no effect. Therefore, it is crucial for dancers to pursue personal definition. We all have a unique calling and purpose for our dance which can be lost, manipulated, or destroyed if we do not seek God to know who we are.

Definition brings you into the power of your identity where:

- ✓ You know who you are
- ✓ You know your purpose, function, and operation
- ✓ You know what God has called you to do and why
- ✓ You know how you should be treated and how your gift should be used. You have a standard for how people should honor what God has placed on the inside of you

We cannot be defined by:

1. **People -** how they view us, how they treat us, what they think of us and what they believe they may know about our ministry.
2. **Religion and tradition -** modes that have been previously set in the past that have established rules, regulations, and bounds on what dance ministry is for and how it should and should not be utilized. Boundaries that have been set in place by lack of revelation and a "this is how it's always been done so this is how it should continue to be done" mind frame.
3. **Our interactions -** harmful interactions with those who do not have the knowledge and revelation of who we are. We should always remain integral and stand in the truth of who we know we are and not settle for anything less. Be quick to forgive and cleanse from any offense or wounds so they do not settle and become a demonic root that perverts our pure identity.

Nothing and nobody but God can define us.

> ***Jeremiah 31:33*** *But this shall be the covenant that I will make with the house of Israel; after those day, saith the Lord, I will put my law in their inward parts, and write it in their hearts; and will be their God, and they shall be my people.*

This was God writing upon the people of Israel and putting in them identity and definition of who they were and how they should be. This set clear instruction of who they were and who's they were and gave them an outline to follow as he wrote upon them.

The scripture says he put his law in their inward parts.

Put in the Strong's Concordance in this scripture means:

1. To give
2. Ascribe, apply, assign
3. Bestow, cast forth, charge
4. Commit, distribute, set forth, ordain

When God put his law in them, he gave it to them like an inheritance. He ordained and set them forth in his law. He ascribed it to them, attributing it as belonging to them as qualities and characteristics. This passage is a clear display of God giving definition and identity.

The scripture then says and I will write it in their hearts.

Write in the Strong's Concordance in this scripture means:

1. To inscribe, engrave, enrol
2. Describe in writing
3. To decree, be recorded, to be written on

He wrote in their hearts which is the inner man, the emotions, the will, the mind, the thoughts, the soul, the knowledge, the intellect, the memory, the conscience, the moral character. He wrote in the deep places of their nature such that it would be impressed deeply. He put a literal description of who they were inside of them. They were like a full book that had been scribed by God. The law is the word of God, and Jesus is the Word (John 1). As God put his law in the people and inscribed it upon their hearts, he was putting himself inside of them, giving them

His DNA. They were identified as being his people, as he said I will be their God and they will be my people.

In Matthew 16:13-20, Peter communicates his revelation of Jesus' true identity. After he shares his revelation, Jesus identifies Peter and gives him definition.

Matthew 16:13-20 *When Jesus came into the coasts of Caesarea Philippi, he asked his disciples, saying, Whom do men say that I the Son of man am? And they said, Some say that thou art John the Baptist: some, Elias; and others, Jeremias, or one of the prophets. He saith unto them, But whom say ye that I am? And Simon Peter answered and said, Thou art the Christ, the Son of the living God. And Jesus answered and said unto him, Blessed art thou, Simon Barjona: for flesh and blood hath not revealed it unto thee, but my Father which is in heaven. And I say also unto thee, That thou art Peter, and upon this rock I will build my church; and the gates of hell shall not prevail against it. And I will give unto thee the keys of the kingdom of heaven: and whatsoever thou shalt bind on earth shall be bound in heaven: and whatsoever thou shalt loose on earth shall be loosed in heaven. Then charged he his disciples that they should tell no man that he was Jesus the Christ.*

From this scriptural passage, we learn that revelation of who you are does not come from flesh and blood, meaning it does not come through natural means. It comes through spiritual revelation. God conveyed to Peter the identity of Jesus that he was the Christ, Son of the living God. None of the other people were right, but the one who had revelation from the Father could accurately distinguish the true identity of Jesus. People will be wrong about who you are, things will be wrong, your interactions will be wrong, but revelation from God will always be right about who you are. After Peter states the truth of Jesus, Jesus then begins to bring definition to Peter.
He says:

You are Peter, my rock - calling him by name and decreeing out the meaning of his name.

I will build my church upon the rock and the gates of hell shall not prevail against it - declaring I will establish my vision on you and on the firm foundation of my defining of you. Hell will not prevail against it. Hell knows who you are, but it cannot conquer over who I say you are and what I build on you.

I will give you the keys of the kingdom of heaven, and whatever you bind on earth shall be bound in heaven, and whatever you loose on earth shall be loosed in heaven - I give you unlimited access and governing authority in heaven, in the earth, and all realms that I have called you too.

Jesus clearly defines Peter and his ministry. He imparts it to him and tells him of the power and authority he has to walk in it. My God! When God writes on you, he gives a full download of revelation and does not leave you empty of the power you need to accomplish it. He establishes his word in you and God's word does not return void. It accomplishes each thing that it is set out to do.

The defining of God will shift you into full revelation of who you are and the purpose of your ministry. Established definition will deliver you from identity hindrances, destruction, and mixture while elevating you to the highest peak of your God given power and authority. Your establishing is like an authoritative decree being released. Job 22:28 says "*Thou shalt also decree a thing, and it shall be established unto thee: and the light shall shine upon thy ways.*" When a decree is released, it must be established and God then shines light upon it.

Ways in the Strong's Concordance in this scripture means:

■	■
☐ A road	☐ Manner, habit
☐ A course of life or mode of action	☐ Of course of life
☐ Journey, path direction	☐ Of moral character

Light in the Strong's Concordance in this scripture means:

■	■
☐ Illumination	☐ Light of prosperity
☐ Light of lamp	☐ Light of instruction
☐ Light of life	☐ Light of face

Enlightenment of who you are follows as you become established in the definition of God for your life. Your path is illuminated and unveiled. Your course of life, journey, and direction is spotlighted and revealed. God shines his light that opens a pathway for you to be able to obtain it. As a dancer, it is important to have enlightenment of who you are in the totality of your life, as this gives greater clarity and purpose to your dance beyond being a gift from God.

My translation of this scripture is:

Nina's Translation *Decree who you are in God and you will be established. The light of God will shine on you bringing illumination, revelation, and enlightenment to all that encompasses your preordained and predefined destiny path and course of life in God.*

Through a decree, you put law and government behind your definition to enforce it (as *decree* in dictionary.com means a formal and authoritative order, especially one having the force of law). You become legalized, authorized, recognized, and protected by law, official, valid, and warranted of acknowledgment. Legal rights, privileges, and advantages are established. With this revelation in mind, a dance minister who lacks understanding of their definition in God, is illegal.

Some of the synonyms of *illegal* are bootleg, criminal, crooked. When you are not defined, you are like a criminal. Your actions are identical to one who is lying and being deceiving, as even though you may be unaware of your actions, you are not displaying the truth of who you are. You will be operating in a bootleg crooked version of you, thus causing your dance to be bootleg as it is not exuding from authenticity. Your ministry will not be as effective as God purposed it to be since you are not operating in your true authorized identity. His covering will not be with you as you are not positioned in his design and all types of warfare and attacks will have access to you.

> ***Acts 19:13-16 New International Version*** *Some Jews who went around driving out evil spirits tried to invoke the name of the Lord Jesus over those who were demon-possessed. They would say, "In the name of Jesus whom Paul preaches, I command you to come out." Seven sons of Sceva, a Jewish chief priest, were doing this. One day the evil spirit answered them, "Jesus I know, and Paul I know about, but who are you?" Then the man who has the evil spirit jumped on them and overpowered them all. He gave them such a beating that they ran out of the house naked and bleeding.*

This passage of scripture is a depiction of what it looks like to operate illegally, unauthorized, and without any protection by God's law. The seven sons of Sceva were operating out of a place of familiarity and not out of the authentic identity and definition of who they were. They saw the use of the name of Jesus and how it had been powerful in casting out devils, so they tried to do the same thing without having any true revelation. They had no knowledge of or relationship with the giver of the power and authority

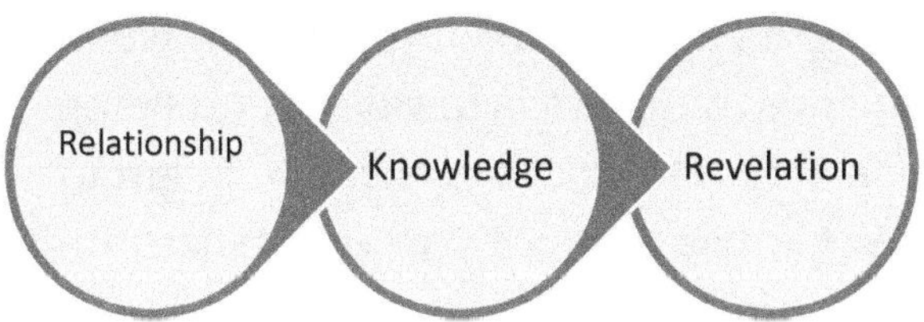

If we do not take the time to come into our authentic identity, we are liable to operate from a place of familiarity because there is no true revelation of who we are and the purpose of our gift. Although we have acknowledged the fact that a gift is present, power is present, authority is present, we have yet to come into relationship with our identity to access its authenticity. We have not spent time learning about what the gift, power, and authority means to us and how God constructed it to be expressed through us. This results in utilizing our gift of dance illegally with no authorization. Therefore, we have no protection. We are not recognized by demons, or in the realms to which we are trying to operate.

The seven sons of Sceva aimed to cast out the devil by saying, "*In the name of Jesus whom Paul preaches*". They were trying to do ministry through the revelation of who Paul was and his relationship with God, not through the revelation of who they were and their own relationship with God. Then the evil spirit answered and said, "*Jesus I know, and Paul I know about, but who are you?*" They were not recognized by the demons since they had no authorization from God and were operating illegally. Consequently, the demons could legally attack them and did just that.

Dance ministers must know they are designed to be intentional vessels of God with calling, purpose, and power to bring heaven to earth through their movement. The capacity of dance ministers is limitless, and being defined gives you access to discover this and begin to embody it. When God authorizes you as a dance minister, you have legal jurisdiction over the enemy and are recognized in both heavenly and earthly places.

As it pertains to you as a dancer, think about times where you conducted ministry through the revelation, relationship, and research of someone else, rather than your own true understanding of who you are.

After reading this chapter thus far, were there times you were completing ministry assignments and you were experiencing warfare because of lack of true identity definition?

Part 2 Defining Your Ministry

> ***Acts 19:16 English Standard Version*** *Then some of the itinerant Jewish exorcists undertook to invoke the name of the Lord Jesus over those who had evil spirits, saying, "I adjure you by the Jesus whom Paul proclaims." Seven sons of a Jewish high priest named Sceva were doing this. But the evil spirit answered them, "Jesus I know, and Paul I recognize, but who are you?" And the man in whom was the evil spirit leaped on them, mastered all of them and overpowered them, so that they fled out of that house naked and wounded.*

> Acts 19:16 says that the demons "overpowered them all." Dance ministers must know who they are to go to war against demonic powers. Knowing who you are is a source of protection. When we are established legally in identity, demons will not be able to overpower us.

The seven sons of Sceva ran out of the house naked and bleeding! The enemy stripped them of their clothing and left them wounded! They were stripped naturally and spiritually of the false power and authority they had. It was easy for the enemy to uncover them because they were unauthorized. They did not have the covering that comes with walking in true identity and relationship with God. Your true identity mantles you. It is your covering from God and the embodiment of who you are in him which cannot be stripped or taken from you.

In Acts 19:13-16 the demons called Jesus and Paul by their name. As we become legalized and authorized we are identified and recognized by our name.

> ***Isaiah 43:1*** *But now, this is what the Lord, your Creator says, O Jacob, And He who formed you, O Israel, "Do not fear, for I have redeemed you [from captivity]; I have called you by name; you are Mine!*

God delivered us from captivity and legalized it by calling our name. He said I have redeemed you, I have called you by name, so you are legally mine. I can legally save you from captivity because you belong to me. We are identified as being attached to God by our name. This is why we cannot allow any and everything to define and name us. Whatever defines and names you, owns you. You are legally bound to it. If the name of your ministry is "This Little Light of Mine Ministry" you are limited to only producing the little light of God rather than the radiating, illuminating, blazing glory light of God. If the name is "Ladies of Glory Dance Ministry" it will exclude men from being able to be a part. It is okay to have just men's and women's ministries, but only if that is what God ordained and revealed to you as the vision of the ministry. To have members of the opposite sex in a ministry with a name of this nature contradicts the identity and definition that is presented in the name, and could mean that the name was not truly received from God and needs revising.

Your name should be a statement of God's ordained vision and call upon your life. It should be a testament to who you are and it should embody your purpose and identity. It should be a short but powerful detailed description of who you are, and what God has called you to do.

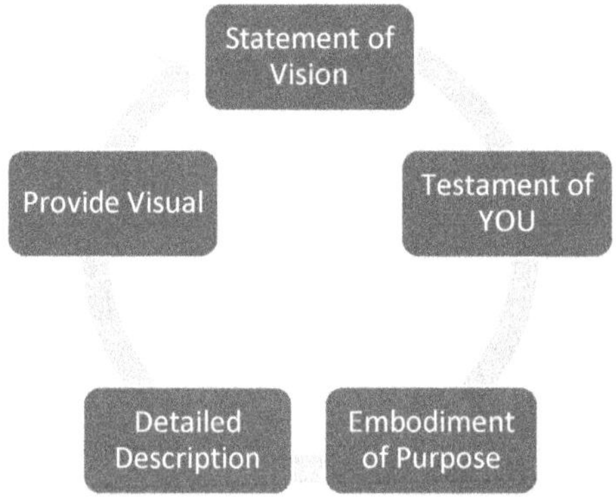

It should provide a quick visual of your definition to the onlooker. If the name of your ministry is "Q & Q Mime," "Up & Down Ministries," "Two & Three Productions," it does not give an adequate description of who you are, what you do, and why you do it; and truly there is no power and authority behind it. You cannot even tell that it is a godly group besides the words "ministry" placed behind it. Your name should have the nature and spirit of God infused into it, and if it does not, it will show who you and your ministry belong too. If the name of your ministry is "The Juking Astral Group" we know it is not God, and if it is "Witches for Jesus" we for sure know that it is not God! These are blatant examples, but it is so key that we grasp this revelation and pay attention to what we name our ministries. It can either help elevate, platform and cover us, or it can be our downfall and cause of lack and exposure.

Your name shows who you belong to.

As you establish your name, is it established on earth, in heaven, and in hell, and demons know who you are. Your name gives you power over them because you are positioned in the authority and revelation of who you are. Through the understanding of your name, you know how to operate in its purposes and skills. You are confident and bold in who you are and demons must respond.

> ***Philippians 2:9-10*** *Wherefore God also hath highly exalted him, and given him a NAME which is above every NAME: That at the NAME of Jesus every knee should bow, of things in heaven, and things in earth, and things under the earth;*

Jesus' NAME gives him authority, power, and recognition in all realms. Every knee bows at the name Jesus, in heaven, in the earth, and under the earth. When you name your ministry, you gain authority and power in the realms that God has granted to your hands. Your regions, territories, and entire spheres of influence must bow and be subject to your influence.

Exalt in the Strong's Concordance in this scripture means:

1. To elevate above others
2. Raise to the highest position
3. Highly exalt

4. To exalt to the highest rank and power, raise to supreme majesty

Some of the definitions of *exalt* in Dictionary.com are "*to raise in rank, honor, power, character, quality, elevate*." Your name elevates you, gives you rank, and lifts you to your highest position in God. It raises you to the highest honor and endowment. The name itself provides a platform in the spirit realm because it automatically exalts you in your purpose and identity. It exalts you above anything that tries to thwart and taint your purpose and make you be anything less. It raises you to the position God ordained for you, and even if you are not ready to walk in it, you inherit it because it is your God-given identity. Your name is given, you do not earn it. IT'S WHO YOU ARE! God's platform is given as inheritance and ordination, as it is where he places you. It is not earned by you, or by man's perception and ability which is different from what we are taught in the world, and even what the church teaches. We are taught that we have to earn our name. We have to work for it, prove it, perform to show and display it, live up to it, show we are worthy of it, and essentially win it. As a name is inherited and given to you, it is given simply because of the nature of who you are (this is why you cannot name your ministry until you first know who you are). It is by nature, it cannot be changed, although it can be rejected and forfeited.

One of the definitions of *inherit* in Dictionary.com is to receive a genetic character by the transmission of hereditary factors. Your inherited name is a part of your genes. It is in your DNA, and no outside factor can hinder the expression of that. Naturally, inherited genes are expressed through characteristics, features, physical appearance, and there is no way to erase or hinder these expressions unless with artificial adjustments. This is why people can say you look like your mom or you act like your dad because that is the expression of the DNA you inherited from them. As you spiritually come into the inheritance of your name, there is nothing that can hinder the power, authority, and identity expression of who you are. As you read, write this key down, **your name is not earned, it is inherited. It is simply the nature of who you are.**

Your name is so significant that Jesus said in Luke 10:19-20, *"Look, I have given you authority over all the power of the enemy, and you can walk among snakes and scorpions and crush them. Nothing will injure you. But don't rejoice because evil spirits obey you; rejoice because your NAMES are registered in heaven."*

He said do not rejoice or be focused on the fact that demons are subject to you, rejoice in the fact that your name is registered in heaven. The establishing and appointing of your name is what is most important and all else follows after your identity.

When a baby is born, they cannot create the birth certificate until the baby is named. After you name the baby:

- The decree of who they are can be written and established. This lets us know that without a name you are not established. (Think of this as it pertains to your ministries. If they are not named, they are not established. Having no name is just as detrimental as having a wrong name.)
- You identify who the baby belongs to.
- The existence of the baby is confirmed. Your name confirms you and who you are, and it confirms your purpose.
- The baby is given identity and definition.

Moses name means "drawing out of the water".

Jesus name means "Jehovah is salvation".

Jeremiah's name means "whom Jehovah has appointed".

These names define and identify who they are and what their purpose was.

Many do not know the truth of who we are as dance ministers. We have been performers, entertainers, fillers, outcasts, and disposable in many ways. Used for the special church events and functions to be put on display and be a quick enjoyment for the people. This has exposed wounds as we have shifted into desiring to be used at a greater capacity. For this reason, it is essential that we gain genuine identity definition and revelation, walk in it, and then teach it to others. As we do this, mindsets of dance ministry will begin to change and we will see our influence increase and surpass that of the world's artistic influence.

Some of us are called to pioneer in the revelation and knowledge that God has given us. From dictionary.com *pioneers* are those who are among the first to settle in a region thus opening it up for occupation and development by others, one of a group of foot soldiers detailed to make roads, dig entrenchments and etc. in advance of the main body. Pioneers will help the whole body to advance so the generations that follow can continue developing and going even further.

These are some questions that you should ask yourself as you shift into God's definition for you.

1. Who are you? What has God revealed to you about who you are?

2. What is the name of your ministry, whether you are a part of a group or you minister alone?

3. Why is this the name of your ministry? What is the vision and purpose of your ministry, and is this presented through the name?
4. What are the names of your gifts? What is the meaning and purpose of each of these?

Chapter 2
I AM DECLARATION!

By: Minister Nina Cook

I am a miracle worker!

I work miracles through the administration of my movements!

I am a healer!

The power to heal lives in me!

I can speak a thing and healing comes!

Power resides in my body through His spirit and the embodiment of the word!

I carry his voice, like the sound of thunder and the roar of rushing waters!

I am the fountain of God, I flow by his spirit, I live, move, breathe, and have my very own being in him!

I am inserted in him and he is inserted in me. He is not just a piece of me but he is the whole of me, and the whole of my ministry!

I am an open well of God I never run dry, because he has open access to flow freely through me!

God's liberty and freedom reigns boundless within me!

I am unlimited, there is no end to me!

God can always speak through me, God can always move through me, God can always use me!

I am a living sacrifice to God, I am holy and acceptable to him!

My body is his temple and his abiding place!

I give a sweet smelling aroma to his nostrils!

I live broken and I live contrite, therefore God will not despise me!

I am humble, yielded and surrendered to his identity, destiny and purposes for me!

His kingdom will be advanced through me, and heaven will come to earth because of me!

I am the manifestation of heaven in the earth, I am the manifestation of his glory!

I am the boldness of God, I can approach his throne in the time of need!

My voice reaches his throne, my prayer reaches his throne, my dance reaches his throne and I receive results!

I am a results producer!

Solutions flow through me into all who receive of me, and into the regions that I influence!

I am a change maker and I am a shift creator!

I am the embodiment of a kingdom shifter!

Change follows me, shift follows me. They are my birthing partners!

My dance pushes out transformational fruit!

There is nothing that cannot change and will not shift because of me!

I am breakthrough, the spirit of the breaker rest upon me!

My dance breaks chains and demonic strongholds!

I am the warclub of God and his weapon of mass destruction!

I thrash demonic kingdoms into pieces of worthless matter!

As I move with the power and authority of God, I remove those things which can be shaken because I am sent from the unshakeable kingdom!

Things have to move because of me, I am the move of God!

Like Jesus I am the word of God, and like the word, I am fire and like the hammer that breaks the rock in pieces!

I am an annihilator, when I stand in who I am, darkness of the enemy disintegrates and dissolves before me!

I am not scared, I do not have the spirit of fear, but power, love, and a sound mind!

I am fearless, and dauntless, there is no flinch in me. I have set my face like flint, like stone I am determined to do his will and I know I will not be put to shame!

I am fierce and have the pursuit of a lion. I pursue my enemies and overtake them, I do not turn back till they are destroyed!

I will not be turning back, I am all in, I am all in my purpose, all in my destiny, all in my calling, and God is all in me!

He has taught my hands to war and my fingers to fight, I am like David I slay Goliaths!

I am a skilled warrior and a skilled marksmen, I do not miss my target!

I am sharp, smart, quick, and wise. I am not ignorant to the devils devices so I conquer in everything that concerns me!

I conquer in my family, I conquer in my region, I conquer in my life and destiny!

God gives me power so even mountains are made low because of me. I tell them to be cast into the sea and they go!

There is nothing too big or complex for me, and there are no walls in heaven or on earth that can hinder me!

When I move, I run through troops and leap over walls!

My feet are like hinds' feet!

I am able to stand firmly and make progress on the dangerous heights of testing and trouble!

God sets me securely upon my high places and has given me plenty of room for my steps under me that my feet would not slip!

In my dance, I have a ferocious pursuit!

I overtake my enemies and do not turn back until they are consumed!

I smite them so that they are not able to rise. They fall wounded under my feet!

For God girds and mantles me with strength for each battle!

My enemies are subdued under me and they are bowed in terror of the almighty God alive and active within me!

I am ordained by God and called forth for this time!

The full armor of God covers me!

The belt of truth, breastplate of righteousness, shoes on my feet having put on the readiness given by the gospel of peace, the shield of faith extinguishing the flaming darts of the enemy, the helmet of salvation, and the sword of the spirit which is the word!

I am completely covered and distinctly mantled for my ministry!

I am God's creation and design!

His blueprint and his handiwork!

His embroidery, elaboration, and embellishment!

He has made me perfectly. I am his ornament!

His image, replica and fruit of his being!

All of creation is eagerly waiting for the manifestation and revealing of me, the carrier of His glory!

Power of Declaration

This is a declaration that I wrote after God gave me the revelation on the importance of being defined. I released it at the 2016 Manifold Grace Production of "Who Am I", and it was empowering and shifting within the region and every person who received of it. I decree the fullness of this impartation is coming upon you now in Jesus name. I decree you are shifting into stronger confidence, boldness, fearlessness, fierceness, power and authority, and in being reckless, destructive, and ferocious against the enemy as you go forward in your ministry.

Written declarations that you can speak over yourself serve as an effective tool to deposit in your spirit that which God has revealed about your identity, definition and who you have been called to be. I have written a countless number of decrees in my journal based on what

God is speaking to me for certain seasons. Writing them down scribes and impresses them inside of me and within the earth realm, and it provides me with an applicable weapon that I can use as necessary through my walk with God. During my prayer time or personal time with the Lord, I recite them with authority over myself and sometimes I use my prayer language to further engrave it within my soul and spirit. The fruit of this becomes immediately evident and tangible both inwardly- in my character, confidence, personality, and outwardly- as I minister and pour out to others. It is much like the shaping and sculpting of a child when a parent recites to them that they are beautiful, loved, and smart. This creates a healthy sense of identity, definition, confidence, and self-esteem within them. Declarations help to sculpt and shape us in what God thinks of us, and it births out the manifestation of his design that has already been present since our birth. They appeal to our nature while drawing out our authenticity, much like a call and response occurrence. We call out the truth of our identity, and the truth of our identity within resurrects and responds.

After reading this declaration, I want to encourage you to write your own concerning who you are and what God has revealed to you about your definition and identity. I will even prick you to begin to make writing declarations a habit and practice of your life and journey in the Lord. Your vocabulary and understanding of who you are and what God works in you throughout the different seasons of your life will grow immensely. Study of the word of God, increased knowledge of the scripture, and the authority and power of your prayer life will be emphatically affected by your declarations. The fruit of each specific and tailor made decree will be abundant and evident. I have made this a practice and discipline of my life and the results have changed my life, my ministry, my dance, my character and nature, my personality, and my confidence. Shift and start today! Maybe even right now when you put this chapter down.

The written declaration does not have to sound like a poem, or have a lyrical flow. Some of my declarations come forth in the form of a poem, while others are more like a list. Either of these are sufficent, it just needs to be clear, concise, authoritative, and filled with the truth and word of God. God can manifest something different and unique through you as you write. Be open to however God leads, directs and inspires you. Remember, these declarations are tailor made. Many times, I use scripture as the foundational basis of the declarations that I write. When God is speaking to me on a particular topic, I will seek God to lead me to scripture that reveal this within his word. The scripture foundation develops into an authoritative decree that is personal to me or whoever God is directing me to decree over. When in prayer or communion with God, he may also speak candidly. For example, he may say "I have called you as my prayer warrior", and "You are my servant leader." When this happens, I tend to immediately jot down what he says and this may form into a list declaration. Poem declarations can be added to and revised, but list declarations can be expanded for years and years. In 2014, I began a list entitled "Who I Am in the Lord." It began in a time of prayer and God told me to keep adding to it through the years as he continued expanding my identity and calling. I will probably be adding to this list until I go to glory in heaven, and then the generations after me will be able to receive its impartation. I started with about ten points in 2014, and now in 2017 three years later it has grown to 67 points and counting of truths about my identity and calling. Each time God leads me to declare it over myself, I am further empowered and filled with its truth. It has created a foundational basis for my identity in God that I can go back to and use as a tool against the enemy during seasons of warfare, and amid times of insecurity and discouragement. Your declarations can be used as a tool in similar fashion and also whatever God may uniquely reveal to you as its purpose in your life and journey. You will be blessed from the fruit yielded as you cultivate yourself in this nature. No points are too small or insignificant to begin to write your decree. Everything that God speaks to you and about you is important, needed, and a part of who you are. It does not have to be an elaborate masterpiece, God will be pleased with your heart to grow in him and further embrace his design in you. Let the declarations begin!

Chapter 3
The Embodiment of the Word of God

By: Minister Nina Cook

Dancers carry the word of God and this is what gives us our effectiveness in ministry. We become the word, and then through movement we release it, preach it, prophesy it, decree and declare it, plant it, establish it, and fruit is produced. Our dance ministry brings forth change because of the power of the word it carries. Therefore, to be effective as dance ministers we must set consistent times to read, study, pray into, apply, and walk in the word of God, such that we become it and carry it within ourselves. When we are preparing to minister in dance, part of this process should include time for seeking God to lead us to scripture that aligns with his will and purpose for that specific ministry assignment. As we study and pray into the scriptures God reveals, every movement will be filled with the potency of the word. This is a part of the mantle and identity of a dancer.

> ***Matthew 4:4*** *But he answered and said, It is written, Man shall not live by bread alone, but by every word that proceedeth out of the mouth of God.*

The word of God is proceeding – it is continuous and eternal. Dancers live on the progressive and excessive word of God. We cannot survive, sustain, or be fruitful without the constant consumption of the word. Dancers must feast on the word of God in order to be effective ministers that produce the kingdom of God in the earth.

> ***Psalm 1:2-3 New International Version*** *but whose delight is in the law of the LORD, and who meditates on his law day and night. That person is like a tree planted*

by streams of water, which yields its fruit in season and whose leaf does not wither – whatever they do prospers.

As we meditate on the word continually, it becomes our foundation and source of prospering.

Psalm 119:11 New International Version *I have hidden your word in my heart that I might not sin against you.*

The word should be hidden in our hearts, a treasure that we store in our inner man, and the wealth to which we regulate our lives.

Acts 6:4 *But we will give ourselves continually to prayer, and to the ministry of the word.*

We must dedicate ourselves to the study of the word and prayer. Prayer is the incubator that molds us into the embodiment of the word. Just like the pastor knows the word, we too must know the word. And even more so, enmesh with it in our very bodies.

John 1:1 *In the beginning was the Word, and the Word was with God, and the Word was God.*

John 1:14 *And the Word was made flesh, and dwelt among us, (and we beheld his glory, the glory as of the only begotten of the Father,) full of grace and truth.*

Jesus was the word personified. His LITERAL flesh was the word! This is the level of embodiment that dancers should be seeking God for. The scripture says that because Jesus was the word in flesh, the word dwelt among us and we beheld his glory full of grace and truth. When you make the word your flesh you are like the word of God dwelling and moving in the earth. As you go forth before the people, they will see the glory of God through you, and you will be the embodiment of his manifest presence, grace, and truth. They should feel as though God has just come into the room when you dance. This is not to say that the people are seeing you as God. This is to say that the glory, grace, truth, and presence of God overshadowing you will be so powerful and evident, that they will see God manifesting through the word you carry. You bring the word to life and give the people a chance to see and receive of the word of God in a way that they have never done so before.

The word of God is your productive ability.

> ***Genesis 1:3*** *And* **God said**, *Let there be light: and there was light.*
>
> ***Genesis 1:6*** *And* **God said**, *Let there be a firmament in the midst of the waters, and let it divide the waters from the waters.*
>
> ***Genesis 1:9*** *And* **God said**, *Let the waters under the heaven be gathered together unto one place, and let the dry land appear: and it was so.*
>
> ***Genesis 1:11*** *And* **God said**, *Let the earth bring forth grass, the herb yielding seed, and the fruit tree yielding fruit after his kind, whose seed is in itself, upon the earth: and it was so.*
>
> ***Genesis 1:14*** *And* **God said**, *Let there be lights in the firmament of the heaven to divide the day from the night; and let them be for signs, and for seasons, and for days, and years:*
>
> ***Genesis 1:20*** *And* **God said**, *Let the waters bring forth abundantly the moving creature that hath life, and fowl that may fly above the earth in the open firmament of heaven.*

***Genesis* 1:24** *And* **God said**, *Let the earth bring forth the living creature after his kind, cattle, and creeping thing, and beast of the earth after his kind: and it was so.*

Genesis 1:26 *And* **God said**, *Let us make man in our image, after our likeness: and let them have dominion over the fish of the sea, and over the fowl of the air, and over the cattle, and over all the earth, and over every creeping thing that creepeth upon the earth.*

***Genesis* 1:28** *And God blessed them, and* **God said** *unto them, Be fruitful, and multiply, and replenish the earth, and subdue it: and have dominion over the fish of the sea, and over the fowl of the air, and over every living thing that moveth upon the earth.*

***Genesis* 1:29** *And* **God said**, *Behold, I have given you every herb bearing seed, which is upon the face of all the earth, and every tree, in the which is the fruit of a tree yielding seed; to you it shall be for meat.*

The main point in each of these scriptures is "**God said**!" Each thing that God said came forth immediately. As dancers who embody what God has said, there is nothing that cannot be produced through your ministry. There is an immediate anointing that comes with the embodiment of the word, so fruit will be produced through you immediately when you carry it at this magnitude. The people and regions that you minister to will immediately be changed and shifted by the will and word of God proclaiming his kingdom from within you.

***Hebrews* 4:12** *For the word of God is quick, and powerful, and sharper than any twoedged sword, piercing even to the dividing asunder of soul and spirit, and of the joints and marrow, and is a discerner of the thoughts and intents of the heart.*

Quick

1. To live, be alive
2. To live, breath, be among the living (not lifeless, not dead)
3. To enjoy real life
4. To have true life and worthy of the name
5. Active, blessed, endless in the kingdom of God
6. In the manner of living and acting- of mortals of character
7. Living water, having vital power in itself and exerting the same upon the soul
8. To be full in vigour, to be fresh strong, efficient,
9. Active, powerful, effacious

Powerful

1. Active, operative, effectual, powerful

As we embody the word it is alive, active, breathing, efficient, powerful and strong through our dance.

Sharper

1. To cut; more comprehensive or decisive than, as if by a single stroke; whereas that implies repeated blows, like hacking
2. More keen, sharper

Dancers who embody the word are precise, exact, direct, keen, and skilled. They do not hack away at the lives of the people and the regions that they dance in with movements that do not have any purpose or revelation. Their movements are like single, sharp, keen, and intentional strokes.

Two-edged

1. Double-edged- with two edges
2. Having a double mouth as a river
3. Used of the edge of the sword and of other weapons, so as the meaning of two-edged

Sword

1. War, judicial, punishment
2. A large knife, used for killing animals and cutting up flesh
3. A small sword distinguished from a large sword
4. Curved sword, for a cutting stroke
5. A straight sword for thrusting

Dancers who embody the word are like swords and exact-o knives. They are like strategic swords formed in a specific way that is most effective in cutting away what is not of God in the people and regions they minister in.

Piercing

1. To reach through
2. Penetrate, pierce, to go through

Dancers who embody the word can reach and pierce through the hearts and minds of the people and the regions they minister to by the power of the active word. Your movements penetrate like a sword doing a work of deliverance, healing, and cleansing that breaks people and regions free from demonic oppression and bondages that have taken residence in them.

You can do a silent work in people through your dance movement by entering their hearts, minds, and regions undetected from the enemy, and from people who are resistant to your ministry. They think they are just sitting in the pew watching and partaking of your ministry, but the embodiment of God's word in you has infiltrated as a dancing intercessor, piercing into their inner man. Through the preciseness of his word, you are healing them, delivering them, and stripping them of all that is not like God.

This is a revelation that should be taught to those who receive of our ministry, such that they can have more knowledge and understanding of the power and operations of our dance ministry. With this knowledge, they will begin to recognize our importance, stop viewing us as sources of entertainment and program fillers, and see us as healers and deliverers.

> ***Isaiah 55:11*** *So shall my word be that goeth forth out of my mouth: it shall not return unto me void, but it shall accomplish that which I please, and it shall prosper in the thing whereto I sent it.*

As you embody the word, it helps you accomplish your destiny, while fully establishing your ministry and purpose where generations glean from the mantle on your life. The word of God always accomplishes, executes, and yields fruit. Therefore, as dancers of the word, your ministry should always yield produce. The word *Void* in the Strong's Concordance means "*empty, in vain, and without cause.*" As a dancer if you do not have any word in you, your dance will be empty, ineffectual, and of no cause. Thus, it will not accomplish or establish anything. It might be a temporary blessing to the people who receive of it, but it will not establish a lasting or eternal work in their lives and regions. As an embodiment of the word, you are like a portal for God to release his word through, then after the word is released, it does the work for you as it prospers in what it was purposed to do. Since the strength and power of the word is accomplishing and establishing through you, as you dance, you can rest in the power and effectiveness of the word and not in your own strength, talent, or abilities.

> ***Jeremiah 1:12*** *Amplified Version Then the LORD said to me, "You have seen well, for I am [actively] watching over My word to fulfill it."*

God will be present with you as you are ministering because he will be watching over the word you embody so he can fulfill it in the people and regions you minister to. He will be looking for a chance to deposit his word, and because you will be full of it, he will be abundantly able to produce it through you.

The word through dance brings...

> ***Psalms 107:20*** *He sent his word, and healed them, and delivered them from their destructions.*

- Healing and deliverance

> ***Jeremiah 23:29*** *Is not my word like as a fire? saith the LORD; and like a hammer that breaketh the rock in pieces?*

- Fire and breakthrough

> ***Psalm 119:130*** *The entrance of thy words giveth light; it giveth understanding unto the simple.*

- Illumination and understanding

> ***Psalm 33:4*** *For the word of the LORD is right; and all his works are done in truth.*

- Righteousness and truth

Psalm 119:105 *Thy word is a lamp unto my feet, and a light unto my path.*

- Guidance and direction

Proverbs 2:6 *For the LORD giveth wisdom: out of his mouth cometh knowledge and understanding.*

- Wisdom, knowledge, and understanding

Isaiah 40:8 *The grass withereth, the flower fadeth: but the word of our God shall stand for ever.*

Matthew 24:35 *Heaven and earth shall pass away, but my words shall not pass away.*

- Produces an eternal work

Hebrews 1:3 *The Son is the radiance of God's glory and the exact representation of his being, sustaining all things by his powerful word. After he had provided purification for sins, he sat down at the right hand of the Majesty in heaven.*

- Sustainability and preservation

Psalm 119:9 *Amplified Version How can a young man keep his way pure?*
By keeping watch [on himself] according to Your word [conforming his life to Your precepts].

- Purity and conformity with the precepts of God

John 7:38 *He that believeth on me, as the scripture hath said, out of his belly shall flow rivers of living water.*

- Salvation and the holy spirit

Psalm 56:4 *In God, whose word I praise; In God I have put my trust; I shall not fear. What can mere man do to me?*

- Empowerment, confidence, and trust

  Matthew 7:24 *English Standard Version Everyone then who hears these words of mine and does them will be like a wise man who built his house on the rock.*

- Foundation and stability

Chapter 4
BECOMING GOD'S WEAPON OF MASS DESTRUCTION

By: Apostle Taquetta Baker

There is a dimension of dance ministry where the dancer can become a literal weapon of mass destruction. Through scripture, your body and movements can be used as a warfare instrument to confound the wise and confound the devil.

> **1Corinthians 1:27** *But God hath chosen the foolish things of the world to confound the wise; and God hath chosen the weak things of the world to confound the things which are mighty.*
>
> **2Corinthians 10:4-6** *(For the weapons of our warfare are not carnal, but mighty through God to the pulling down of strong holds;) Casting down imaginations, and every high thing that exalteth itself against the knowledge of Godand bringing into captivity every thought to the obedience of Christ; And having in a readiness to revenge all disobedience, when your obedience is fulfilled.*

When God confounds the enemy, he uses unique - unassuming weapons to confuse, shame, dishonor, disgrace, repulse, awe, dismantle, refute, damn, defeat, and overthrow the enemy.

King David, a mighty warrior and worshipper, danced naked, liberated, and abandoned before God. His dance was so confounding until his wife who should have known his character and supported him, was in awe and appalled by his actions. David's dance judged a demonic spirit in her such that her womb was shut and she never had children. David's dance was such a weapon of mass destruction that it cut off his own lineage through a wife who could not understand and respect his dance ministry unto the Lord.

> ***2 Samuel 6:13-16*** *And it was so, that when they that bare the ark of the Lord had gone six paces, he sacrificed oxen and fatlings. And David danced before the Lord with all his might; and David was girded with a linen ephod. So, David and all the house of Israel brought up the ark of the Lord with shouting, and with the sound of the trumpet. And as the ark of the Lord came into the city of David, Michal Saul's daughter looked through a window, and saw king David leaping and dancing before the Lord; and she despised him in her heart.*

> ***Versus 20-23*** *Then David returned to bless his household. And Michal the daughter of Saul came out to meet David, and said, how glorious was the king of Israel to day, who uncovered himself to day in the eyes of the handmaids of his servants, as one of the vain fellows shamelessly uncovereth himself! And David said unto Michal, it was before the Lord, which chose me before thy father, and before all his house, to appoint me ruler over the people of the Lord, over Israel: therefore will I play before the Lord. And I will yet be more vile than thus, and will be base in mine own sight: and of the maidservants which thou hast spoken of, of them shall I be had in honour. Therefore Michal the daughter of Saul had no child unto the day of her death.*

The word dance in this scripture means "*to whirl*." David was dancing in violent abandonment unto the Lord. He called his own dance "*vile*." He knew it was foolish, confusing, and confounding to people and the devil, yet glorifying to God.

I believe David recognized the power of his dance and that it annihilated his enemies and the enemies of God. Why do I believe this???? I am glad you asked. David wrote the book of Psalms. In Psalms 149, he mentions a dance of praise that executes vengeance upon the heathen, punishments upon the people who are against God, binds demonic kings with chains, and their nobles with fetters of iron, while executing upon them the judgment written. According to this Psalms, all saints have the honor and ability of the Lord to display this dimension of praise where it destroys the enemy.

> ***Psalms 149:3-9*** *Let them praise his name in the dance: let them sing praises unto him with the timbrel and harp. For the Lord taketh pleasure in his people: he will beautify the meek with salvation. Let the saints be joyful in glory: let them sing aloud upon their beds. Let the high praises of God be in their mouth, and a twoedged sword in their hand; To execute vengeance upon the heathen, and punishments upon the people; To bind their kings with chains, and their nobles with fetters of iron; To execute upon them the judgment written: this honour have all his saints. Praise ye the Lord.*

The word execute insinuates that we are carrying out a mission or specific assignment according to a law or a particular purpose. Per Dictionary.com, execute also means, "*to inflict capital punishment on, put to death according to law, to murder, to assassinate.*" When we operate as weapons of mass destruction, we have specific assignments of releasing vengeance and judgment on enemies and wickedness. We are also exacting punishment through our movements. When we exact punishment, we are bringing rebuke, reproof, correction, chastisement, and reasoning. We are expressing disapproval and scolding the enemy and wickedness for their actions. Bind is an act of imprisonment. As a weapon of mass destruction, you are not imprisoning little demons or those who engage in minor sins. Nobles and kings are principalities and ruling demons and people that have great powers. You cannot be a wimpy dancer to attack these realms of demonic influence. You must be a weapon of mass destruction so that when you attack, these principalities and ruling powers are destroyed, where they cannot impact the lives of people or defy God anymore. This is the mindset of one who is a weapon of God.

We can quickly discern the destructive power of worldly dance, but we do not pursue, activate, or embrace this destructive power in our spiritual dance ministries. Salmone, Herodias daughter's dance was such a weapon of mass destruction for the devil until the King Herod was like "*ask what you will and I will grant it.*" Her dance was so confounding that she warranted the beheading of John the Baptist.

> ***Matthew 14: 3-12*** *For Herod had laid hold on John, and bound him, and put him in prison for Herodias' sake, his brother Philip's wife. For John said unto him, it is not lawful for thee to have her. And when he would have put him to death, he feared the multitude, because they counted him as a prophet. But when Herod's birthday was kept, the daughter of Herodias danced before them, and pleased Herod. Whereupon he promised with an oath to give her whatsoever she would ask. And she, being before instructed of her mother, said, Give me here John Baptist's head in a charger. And the king was sorry: nevertheless, for the oath's sake, and them which sat with him at meat, he commanded it to be given her. And he sent, and beheaded John in the prison. And his head was brought in a charger, and given to the damsel: and she brought it to her mother. And his disciples came, and took up the body, and buried it, and went and told Jesus.*

Salome asked for John the Baptist's head as a charger. This was her payment for her seductive dance. It was also a cleverly crafted executed judgment, as her mother instructed her to ask for John the Baptist's head. John the Baptist was a famous prophetic preacher that paved the way for Jesus to be revealed as savior. King Herod had already imprisoned John the Baptist for rebuking him regarding divorcing his wife and marrying his brother's wife Herodias. Herodias did not like this reproof even though it was the law. She executed a demonic plan and exacted her own judgment against John the Baptist. Her judgment was not justifiable, but a binding contract in the form of a verbal agreement was released when King Herod promised to give Salome whatever she wanted as payment for her dance. Her dance was a weapon of mass destruction that fulfilled the judgement through the King's verbal binding. Even though it was not written naturally, it was spiritual inscribed in the heavenlies, and was a verbal agreement among both parties. Therefore, it was comparable to a written law. Moreover, people witnessed the verbal vow, so King Herod had to keep it to maintain his integrity and authority. Salome released a dance where King Herod spoke without considering the ramifications of his words. He was baffled, in awe, seduced, and confounded. This is the reason God does not want us to dance for the devil and the world. We can tap into dimensions of movement where there is destroying power in our dance. It is a power of mass destruction that God placed inside of us, not to defy him, but to destroy the enemy.

We see so many dance ministers mimicking the world, yet not realizing that their dance can have grave impact if it is not done through the well of the Lord and unto the Lord. Ecclesiastes 1:4 reveals to us that there is an appointed time to dance. I believe the Lord warned us of this because of the power of our dance. If you dance at the wrong time and for the wrong reasons, you can be a weapon of mass destruction unto people, their lives, destinies, and lineages, and even unto your own self. We further see this with Jephthah's daughter in Judges 11:30-31. Jephthah made a vow that if God enabled him to win the battle against the children of Ammon, he would offer a sacrifice of whatever came before him when he returned home from the war.

> ***Verse 11:30-31*** *And Jephthah vowed a vow unto the Lord, and said, if thou shalt without fail deliver the children of Ammon into mine hands, then it shall be, that whatsoever cometh forth of the doors of my house to meet me, when I return in peace from the children of Ammon, shall surely be the Lord's, and I will offer it up for a burnt offering.*

In verse 34, we find Jephthah's daughter meeting him with the timbrel and dance as he returned from the war. Unlike Salome, Jephthah's daughter's dance was appropriate because it was customary for the women to meet the men with a victory celebration dance when they returned from war. And though she was unaware, her timing was not the best. Since she was the first person to meet her father when he returned from war, he had to keep his vow to the Lord by offering her as a sacrifice. She therefore, had to live undefiled and unmarried, in the temple of the Lord for the rest of her life.

> ***Verse 32-39*** *So Jephthah passed over unto the children of Ammon to fight against them; and the Lord delivered them into his hands. And he smote them from Aroer, even till thou come to Minnith, even twenty cities, and unto the plain of the vineyards, with a very great slaughter. Thus the children of Ammon were subdued before the children of Israel. And Jephthah came to Mizpeh unto his house, and, behold, his daughter came out to meet him with timbrels and with dances: and she was his only child; beside her he had neither son nor daughter. And it came to pass, when he saw*

her, that he rent his clothes, and said, Alas, my daughter! thou hast brought me very low, and thou art one of them that trouble me: for I have opened my mouth unto the Lord, and I cannot go back.

And she said unto him, my father, if thou hast opened thy mouth unto the Lord, do to me according to that which hath proceeded out of thy mouth; forasmuch as the Lord hath taken vengeance for thee of thine enemies, even of the children of Ammon. And she said unto her father, let this thing be done for me: let me alone two months, that I may go up and down upon the mountains, and bewail my virginity, I and my fellows. And he said, Go. And he sent her away for two months: and she went with her companions, and bewailed her virginity upon the mountains. And it came to pass at the end of two months, that she returned unto her father, who did with her according to his vow which he had vowed: and she knew no man. And it was a custom in Israel.

I shared this to signify the importance of governing your dance and your vows unto the Lord. Both are binding weapons of mass destruction. You can dance for good intentions, but at the wrong time, it can be costly. Or you can use your dance for impure intentions like Salome, and lead people astray, all while destroying lives, destinies, and entire lineages.

Like Salome, many people who dance for the devil or in the world, dance to be the best and to destroy anyone who would compete against their dancing ability. The reason we are in awe of them and their ability to produce power and precision in their dance is because they have

- ✓ Practiced - Practice! Practice! Practice!
- ✓ Trained and practiced some more
- ✓ Studied dance

- ✓ Studied dance artists, competitors, and trained some more so they can be better than them
- ✓ Sacrificed their lives, time, and whatever is necessary to equip themselves in their art
- ✓ Made vows and sacrifices to deities in exchange for power and favor to be the best and to be a weapon of mass destruction

They want to live from this dimension. They refuse to come down from this dimension of dance. Settling is not an option for them. And they are not trying to live with their enemies and competitors. They seek to destroy them through their art of dance.

I learned about being a weapon of mass destruction when I was seeking the Lord about a ministry engagement and he told me that our team needed to operate as a weapon of mass destruction. I began to study scriptures on being the weaponry of God, and me and my team began to decree them over our lives and dance ministries. I am going to share the decree in the next chapter. It entails a long list of scriptures of how God uses people as weapons of mass destruction.

- I encourage decreeing these scriptures out loud at least once a week until they become a part of your dance ministry DNA.
- I recommend soaking yourself in the scriptures, while asking God to mold you into a weapon of mass destruction.
- I encourage dancing before the Lord a couple of times a week and asking him to teach you movements and how to move as a weapon of mass destruction.
- I recommend studying deliverance ministry, warfare, intercession, and asking the Lord to teach

you how to tower over darkness and wickedness through dance and ministry in general.

- I recommend seeking God about the principalities and powers that rule in the regions where your church and events are, performing a google study to further map out the history, culture, and spiritual dynamics of the area, seek God about which demonic forces you are to execute judgement on, and to give you the choreographed movements for annihilating the enemy. If you are ministering during praise and worship, then allow the Holy Spirit to lead you in what demonic forces to come against and what movements to minister.

The more you utilize the suggestions above, the more you will become a DAILY dance ministering weapon of mass destruction. But please discern from the above teaching that you must use maturity in governing this realm of ministry.

Chapter 5
WEAPON OF MASS DESTRUCTION DECREE

By: Apostle Taquetta Baker

Becoming A Weapon To Judge High Places & Altars

- ***Psalm 68:21 New Living Bible***: *But God will smash the heads of his enemies, crushing the skulls of those who love their guilty ways.*

  Through me, God is smashing the heads of my enemies. I crush the skulls of demonic forces, judging their wickedness and defiance against God.

- ***Leviticus 26:30 English Standard Bible***: *And I will destroy your high places (regional strongholds) and cut down your incense altars and cast your dead bodies upon the dead bodies of your idols, and my soul will abhor you.*

  I decree I destroy my enemies such that demonic altars are dismantled, sacrifices are demolished, and strongholds die in the region. For just like God, I abhor - hate and despise - wickedness and the counterfeit.

- ***Ezekiel 6:3-4 English Standard Bible:*** *And say, You mountains of Israel, hear the word of the Lord God! Thus says the Lord God to the mountains and the hills, to the ravines and the valleys: Behold, I, even I, will bring a sword upon you, and I will destroy your high places. Your altars shall become desolate, and your incense altars shall be broken, and I will cast down your slain before your idols.*

Oh, mountains of my region and sphere of influence, hear the Word of the Lord! God is making me a mighty sword to destroy your high places. Through me, your altars become desolate, and your incense altars are broken and cast down slain before your idols.

- ***Psalms 21:8-9 English Standard Bible:*** *Your hand will find out all your enemies; your right hand will find out those who hate you. You will make them as a blazing oven when you appear. The Lord will swallow them up in his wrath, and fire will consume them.*

I decree the works of my hands will reveal and expose my enemies, unveil their wicked ways, and their hatred toward me and God. The glory illuminating and working in me, through me, and around me will be like a blazing oven exposing their darkness. Through me, they shall be swallowed up by the Lord's wrath and his Holy Spirit and fire in me will consume them.

God Goes Before Me

- ***Exodus 15:3-6*** *The Lord is a Man of War; the Lord is His name. Your Right Hand, O Lord, has become glorious in power; Your right hand. O Lord, has dashed the enemy in pieces. And in the greatness of Your excellence you have overthrown those who rose against You; You sent forth Your wrath which consumed them like stubble."*

God is a king of war! The Lord is his name! Your right hand of justice is glorious in power! Through me you dash into pieces every enemy. In your excellent greatness, you overthrow all who revolt against you. You send your wrath and consume them as stubble - as chaff and worthless dung.

- ***Isaiah 45:2*** *I will go before you and make the crooked paths straight; I will break in pieces the gates of bronze and cut the bars of iron.*

Thank you Lord that as I minister and live a lifestyle of destiny in you, that you are forever before me, making every crooked path straight; breaking demonic and fortified gates into pieces and cutting through their bronze of iron so that I may have access to all you have for me.

- ***Deuteronomy 9:3*** *Therefore understand today the Lord your God is He who goes before you as a consuming fire. He will destroy them and bring them down before you; so you shall drive them out and destroy them quickly, as the Lord has said to you.*

I fear nothing for I have clear understanding that the Lord goes before me as a consuming fire. Even as I tread in his ordained path, the Lord destroys them that are against me and brings them before me. I follow every word and direction of the Lord as I drive enemies and hindrances out of my sphere of influence. I destroy them quickly so that I can progress forward with the Lord.

<u>Becoming A Fortified City</u>

- ***Jeremiah 1:18-19*** *For, behold, I have made thee this day a defenced city, and an iron pillar, and brasen walls against the whole land, against the kings of Judah, against the princes thereof, against the priests thereof, and against the people of the land. And they shall fight against thee; but they shall not prevail against thee; for I am with thee, saith the Lord, to deliver thee.*

  New Living Bible: *For see, today I have made you strong like a fortified city that cannot be captured, like an iron pillar or a bronze wall. You will stand against the whole land – the kings, officials, priests, and people of Judah (territory). They will fight you, but they will fail. For I am with you, and I will take care of you. I, the Lord, have spoken!"*

  The Amplified Bible: *For I, behold, I have made you this day a fortified city and an iron pillar and bronze walls against the whole land – against the [successive] kings of Judah, against its princes, against its priests, and against the* *people of the land [giving you divine strength which no hostile power can overcome]. And they shall fight against you, but they shall not [finally] prevail against you, for I am with you, says the Lord, to deliver you.*

Defenced is mib̲ṣâr in the Hebrew and means:

1. a fortification, castle, or fortified city
2. figuratively, a defender, (de-, most) fenced, fortress, (most) strong (hold)

Dictionary.com defines *defense* as:

1. resistance against attack; protection
2. something that defends, as a fortification, physical or mental quality, or medication
3. the defending of a cause or the like by speech, argument, etc.
4. a speech, argument, etc., in vindication
5. sports:
   A. the practice or art of defending oneself or one's goal against attack, as in fencing, boxing, soccer, or football.
   B. the team attempting to thwart the attack of the team having the ball or puck.
   C. the players of a team who line up in their own defensive zone.
   D. the positions on the field, ice, etc., taken by such players.

Iron is *barzel* in the Hebrew and means:

1. ax head tool of iron, harshness, strength, oppression
2. iron as cutting, a smith (person who makes and repairs things in iron by hand)

A brazen wall is a bronze, copper, metal or steel wall of protection.

I decree I am your fortified city that cannot be captured, like an iron pillar and a bronze wall. I stand against the whole land - kings, officials, priests, the territory and its strongholds, and the people. They will fight me but I will not fail. For God, you are with me. You take care of me. This is your decree that you have spoken and it shall come to pass for me as I complete your will and specific assignments in the earth.

Becoming A Sharp Instrument

- ***Deuteronomy 33:27 English Standard Bible:*** *The eternal God is your dwelling place, and underneath are the everlasting arms. And he thrust out the enemy before you and said, 'Destroy.'*

  The Lord is my eternal dwelling place. I am encompassed in his everlasting arms. God thrusts out the enemy before me and as he embodies me as his weapon of mass destruction, he says, "DESTROY."

- ***Isaiah 41:15-16*** *Behold, I will make you to be a new, sharp, threshing instrument which has teeth; you shall thresh the mountains and beat them small, and shall make the hills like chaff. You shall winnow them, and the wind shall carry them away, and the tempest or whirlwind shall scatter them. And you shall rejoice in the Lord, you shall glory in the Holy One of Israel.*

  The Amplified Bible: *Behold, I will make thee a new sharp threshing instrument having teeth: thou shalt thresh the mountains, and beat them small, and shalt make the hills as chaff. Thou shalt fan them, and the wind shall carry them away, and the whirlwind shall scatter them: and thou shalt rejoice in the Lord, and shalt glory in the Holy One of Israel.*

I thank you Lord for making me your new, sharp, threshing instrument which has teeth. I thresh the mountains and beat them small, and make the hills like chaff. I winnow them, and the wind carries them away, and the tempest and whirlwind scatters them. I rejoice in the Lord, glorying in the Holy One of Israel for making me a terror to the enemy.

- ***2Chronicles 11:1*** *And when Rehoboam was come to Jerusalem, he gathered of the house of Judah and Benjamin an hundred and fourscore thousand chosen men, which were warriors, to fight against Israel, that he might bring the kingdom again to Rehoboam.*

Lord I am your end-time warrior, you have chosen me and used me as your weapon to fight against and destroy the enemy. Through your works in me, I can bring your kingdom again and again, and again to my region and sphere of influence.

Hands To Shift, Purge & Purify

- ***Matthew 3:12*** *Whose fan is in his hand, and he will throughly purge his floor, and gather his wheat into the garner; but he will burn up the chaff with unquenchable fire.*

  New Living Bible: *His winnowing fan (shovel, fork) is in His hand, and He will thoroughly clear out and clean His threshing floor and gather and store His wheat in His barn, but the chaff He will burn up with fire that cannot be put out.*

Winnowing fan is a winnowing-fork (as scattering like spittle): — fan.

Dictionary.com defines *winnow* as:

1. to free (grain) from the lighter particles of chaff, dirt, etc., especially by throwing it into the air and allowing

the wind or a forced current of air to blow away impurities
2. to drive or blow (chaff, dirt, etc.) away by fanning, to blow upon; fan
3. to subject to some process of separating or distinguishing; analyze critically; sift
4. to separate or distinguish (valuable from worthless parts) (sometimes followed by out): to winnow falsehood from truth
5. to pursue (a course) with flapping wings in flying
6. to fan or stir (the air) as with the wings in flying

Lord I am your winnow fan - your mighty shovel and powerhouse fork. You use me to clear out and clean foundations and purify regions, while giving me discernment of how to gather and store what is of you. I burn up the chaff and the worthless with an unquenchable fire. I multiply that which is Godly through your unquenchable Holy Ghost and Fire.

Becoming An Instrument Of Death

- ***Psalms 7:11-13*** *God judgeth the righteous, and God is angry with the wicked every day. If he turn not, he will whet his sword; he hath bent his bow, and made it ready. He hath also prepared me for himself as an instruments of death; he ordaineth me as his arrows against the persecutors.*

Thank you God for searching and judging me so I can live in righteousness and right standing with you. Even as you are angry with the wicked daily, and prepare to release your sword and bow against those who do not turn from wickedness, prepare me as your instruments of death. I want to kill what defies you Lord. Ordain me as your arrows against the persecutors. I kill that which is not of you and judge that which defies you. I am your instruments of justice in the heavenlies and in the earth.

Becoming A Battle Axe

- ***Jeremiah* 51:20** *Thou art my battle axe and weapons of war: for with thee will I break in pieces the nations, and with thee will I destroy kingdoms.*

  New International Bible: *You are my war club, my weapon for battle-- with you I shatter nations, with you I destroy kingdoms.*

  New Living Bible: *You are my battle-ax and sword," says the LORD. "With you I will shatter nations and destroy many kingdoms.*

  English Standard Bible: *You are my hammer and weapon of war: with you I break nations in pieces; with you I destroy kingdoms.*

  The Message Bible: *God says, You, Babylon, are my hammer, my weapon of war. I'll use you to smash godless nations, use you to knock kingdoms to bits.*

  Battle axe in the Hebrew is Mapes and means, *"a smiter, war club, club, battle axe, hammer."*

  Break in pieces in the Hebrew is *nâp̱as* and mean:
  1. to dash to pieces, or scatter
  2. be beaten in sunder, break (in pieces), broken, cause to be discharged, dispersed, be overspread, scatter
  3. to shatter, shattering, to pulverize, to scatter, disperse, overspread, be scattered, to be scattered, dispersed

JESUS!!!! I am your battle axe, your war club, your club, your hammer, your weapon for battle. With me, you LORD shatter nations! YOU:

- ✓ Dash them in pieces
- ✓ Beat evil and devils to a pulp

- ✓ Beat asunder every defiling and defying entity against your will, purpose, and kingdom
- ✓ You destroy kingdoms
- ✓ Scatter and disperse rulers of darkness, witchcraft, principalities, and powers

Dictionary.com defines *hammer* as:

1. a tool consisting of a solid head, usually of metal, set crosswise on a handle, used for beating metals, driving nails, etc.
2. to fasten by using hammer and nails; nail
3. to shape or ornament (metal or a metal object) by controlled and repeated blows of a hammer; beat out:
4. to produce with or by force
5. to pound or hit forcefully
6. to settle (a strong disagreement, argument, etc.); bring to an end, as by strenuous or repeated effort
7. to present (points in an argument, an idea, etc.) forcefully or compellingly; state strongly, aggressively, and effectively
8. to strike with blows; to make persistent or laborious attempts to finish or perfect something

Dictionary.com defines *pulverize* as:

1. to completely destroy, especially by crushing to fragments or a powder
2. to defeat soundly, thrash
3. to become reduced to powder; to fall to dust

Lord I am your Battle Axe. I am your arm, armament, ammunition, anlace, arbalest, archery, arrow, assegai, atlatl, ax, axe, backsword, ballista, banderilla, barong, bat, baton, battle-ax, bayonet, bazooka, billy club, blackjack, blade, blowgun, bludgeon, bomb, boomerang, bow and arrow, bowie knife, brass knuckles, cannon, catapult, cleaver, club, crossbow, cudgel, cutlass, dagger, dart, dirk, firearm, flamethrower, gun, hammer, harpoon, hatchet, howitzer, hunting knife, knife, lance, machete, machine gun, missile, musket, nerve gas, nuclear bomb, nunchaku, pistol, pulverize, revolver, rifle, saber, scythe, shotgun, slingshot, spear, spike, stiletto, switchblade, sword, tear gas. MY GOD! I am your destroyer! Your weapon of mass destruction! Come on!!!!!!!

Smiting With The Sword Of The Clap

Ezekiel 21:14-17 Thou therefore, son of man, prophesy, and smite thine hands together, and let the sword be doubled the third time, the sword of the slain: it is the sword of the great men that are slain, which entereth into their privy chambers. I have set the point of the sword against all their gates, that their heart may faint, and their ruins be multiplied: ah! it is made bright, it is wrapped up for the slaughter. Go thee one way or other, either on the right hand, or on the left, whithersoever thy face is set. I will also smite mine hands together, and I will cause my fury to rest: I the Lord have said it.

Smite means to strike with a clapping or clasping movement.

Smite is *Naka* in the Hebrew and means:

1. to strike (lightly or severely, literally or figuratively) beat
2. cast forth, clap, give (wounds), go forward, kill, give a thrust
3. make (slaughter), murderer, punish, slaughter, slay(-er, -ing)
4. smite(-r, -ing), strike, be stricken, (give) stripes, surely, wound

I decree I smite my hands and the power of the sword is doubled each time I clap. The sword of my hands is slaying every enemy, it is set at the gates of great men causing their hearts to faint and their ruins to be multiplied. My smite and the claps of my hands is bright and wrapped up to slaughter my enemies on every side. The right, the left, and wherever thy face is set, as I smite my hands my fury is set to rest because I have surely wounded and murdered my enemies.

I decree that with my entire being I prophesy! I am prophecy manifesting! When I clap my hands it is as if the lord of host has rend the sky and caused a shaking and scattering in the earth! When I open my mouth, my words of declarations and high praise unto the lord is like a sword that divides bone and marrow, wheat and tare! My words penetrate the hearts of men and cause them to turn to the father! My words of praise unlocks gates in regions, breaks down walls, and re-establishes hedges of protection!

I decree that as I prophecy my hands are going forth as a double sword activated in heavenly destruction. I declare that with each clap the dunamis power of the Lord is doubling upon my hands. I decree that through God my hands have been registered in the heavenlies to slay even the greatest of men in their secret chambers! Every gate shall come crashing down at the smite of my hands as my very clap shifts them to a point of unconsciousness. I decree a double portion of ruin to come upon every place that my hands will smite bringing mass destruction to every enemy subjected to my hands. My hands are fortified in the glory light of the Lord as they dismantle my enemies to the right and to the left! Peace must be released at the sound of my smite and even the fury of my enemies must bow at the sound of my clap.

I smite with the power of the Lord that causes my enemies to plunder. I decree my hands prophecy a striking sword that murders demonic intel and agents who have set up camps against me. When I prophecy, weapons roll from the womb and birth storehouses of terror to come upon my enemies. My words point swords against their gates causing warriors of darkness to faint. My stance alone prophesies a stripping of their badges. Every step I take my hands multiply their ruin through each generation until the seed will be no more. I decree the Lord speaks to my hands as they war with words of the Lord. My hands prophecy a fury that cannot be laid to rest. I smite with a fury that cause my enemy to dig their own grave. My hands carry nations who hear the sound reverberate from miles away. When I smite I've already won the fight with even the most subtle clap of the hand.

When I clap I prophesy judgement to be released up the head of the enemy. My clap kills every assignment that is contrary to the standard of heaven in my region and sphere of influence. My clap strikes blow upon blow causing every impenetrable gate to fall. Every strike of my clap releases a sound that bellows in ears and hearts of my enemies causing them torment and turn upon themselves slaughtering one another. My clap multiples death upon the enemy and his imps causing utter ruin to every generational assignment. My clap is the light that exposes every hidden places of the enemy and leaves it fruitless and worthless. This clap here is backed by daddy God and is a double edged sword to every enemy that will encounter it.

Becoming The Sword Of God

Hebrews 4:12 For the word of God is quick, and powerful, and sharper than any twoedged sword, piercing even to the dividing asunder of soul and spirit, and of the joints and marrow, and is a discerner of the thoughts and intents of the heart.

Jeremiah 23:9 "Is not My word like fire?" declares the LORD, "and like a hammer which shatters a rock?

We are the word of God made flesh unto men. Dancers and psalmist are the movement and melody of God's word. The word of God through us is

- quick
- powerful
- sharp like a double edge sword
- piercing, intricate, divisive, and decisive
- like fire
- judging and shattering like a hammer
- discerning of thoughts and opinions
- intentional in discerning heart matters

Isaiah 49:2 *And he hath made my mouth like a sharp sword; in the shadow of his hand hath he hid me, and made me a polished shaft; in his quiver hath he hid me.*

Psalms 149:6-9 *Let the high praises of God be in their mouth, and a twoedged sword in their hand; To execute vengeance upon the heathen, and punishments upon the people; To bind their kings with chains, and their nobles with fetters of iron; To execute upon them the judgment written: this honour have all his saints. Praise ye the Lord.*

Sword is *hereb* in the Hebrew and means:

1. drought (cause a shortage, cut off); also a cutting instrument (from its destructive effect)
2. axe, dagger, knife, sword, or other sharp instruments, tool for cutting

3. mattock(an instrument for loosening the soil in digging, shaped like a pickax, but having one end broad instead of pointed)

I decree my movement is the melody of God's word in the earth and in the people I minister too. The word of God through me as I dance is quick, powerful, sharp, piercing, decisive, discerning of thoughts and opinions, intentional in discerning heart matters, like fire, judging and shattering like a hammer against demonic nobles and kings and all that defies God!

Tread Upon The Demonic

Psalms 91:13 *I tread upon the lion and adder, the young lion and dragon I trample under foot.*

Luke 10:19 *I tread upon serpents and scorpions and over all the power of the enemy and nothing shall by any means hurt me.*

Joshua 1:3 *Every place that the sole of your foot shall tread upon, that have I given unto you, as I said unto Moses.*

Tread is *Pateo* in the Greek and means:

1. to trample, crush with the feet, to advance by setting the foot upon, tread upon
2. to encounter successfully the greatest perils from the machinations and persecutions with which Satan would fain thwart the preaching of the gospel
3. to tread under foot, trample on
4. to treat with insult and contempt
5. to desecrate the by devastation and outrage

I decree that my dance treads, tramples, crushes and desecrates the enemy by utter devastation as I move! I tread upon all the power of the enemy and everything that tries to hinder the advancement of the gospel and kingdom of God in the earth. Through the power of my treading alone, I advance the kingdom of God and take up territory for his glory every place the soles of my feet tread.

<u>**Becoming The Finger Of God**</u>

Exodus 8:19 *Then the magicians said to Pharaoh, "This is the finger of God." But Pharaoh's heart was hardened, and he did not listen to them, as the LORD had said. Even devil and wicked people recognize the finger of God.*

Psalms 8:3 *When I consider thy heavens, the work of thy fingers, the moon and the stars, which thou hast ordained; What is man, that thou art mindful of him?*

The works of God's hands produce ordained results.

Luke 11:20 *But if I with the finger of God cast out devils, no doubt the kingdom of God is come upon you.*

The kingdom of God manifests when devils are cast out by the finger of God.

<u>*Cast out* is *ekballō* in the Greek and means:</u>

1. to eject (literally or figuratively), bring forth, cast (forth, out)
2. drive (out), expel, leave, pluck (pull, take, thrust) out, put forth (out)
3. send away (forth, out), with notion of violence, to drive out (cast out)
4. to cast out of the world, i.e. be deprived of the power and influence he exercises in the world
5. to excrement from the belly into the sink, to expel a person from a society: to banish

I decree that my finger embodies the power of the kingdom and has the authority to cast devils out of regions, spheres of influence, atmospheres, nations and people. With my finger, I release swift judgement that drives out, ejects, plucks up, thrust out, and banishes demonic principalities and powers. When I raise my finger, demons and all surely know that the kingdom of God has come upon me.

Battering Ram

***Ezekiel* 4:2-3** *And lay siege against it, and build a fort against it, and cast a mount against it; set the camp also against it, and set battering rams against it round about. Moreover take thou unto thee an iron pan, and set it for a wall of iron between thee and the city: and set thy face against it, and it shall be besieged, and thou shalt lay siege against it. This shall be a sign to the house of Israel.*

Dictionary.com defines Siege as:
a military operation in which enemy forces surround a town or building, cutting off essential supplies, with the aim of compelling the surrender of those inside.

Siege is *Masar* in the Hebrew and means:

1. besieged, bulwark, defence, fenced, fortress, siege, strong (hold)
2. tower. siege- enclosure, siege, entrenchment

Battering Rams is *kar* in the Hebrew and means

1. the sense of plumpness; a ram (as full- grown and fat), including a battering- ram (as butting)
2. hence, a meadow (as for sheep); also a pad or camel's saddle (as puffed out)
3. captain, furniture, lamb, (large) pasture, ram

Dictionary.com defines *battering ram* as:

1. an ancient military device with a heavy horizontal ram for battering down walls, gates, etc.
2. any of various similar devices, usually machine-powered, used in demolition, by police and firefighters to force entrance to a building, etc.

With the battering rams being set up round about, the enemy is continually being hit from every side.

I decree that my dance is like a siege that fences the enemy in, starving him and his demonic assignments of all its resources. My movements are like a military device that batters him over and over again until he surrenders!

Leaping To Breakthrough!
Psalms 18:29 *For by You I can run through a troop, and by my God I can leap over a wall.*

The Message Bible *I smash the bands of marauders, I vault the highest fences.*

Troop is *gedûd* in the Hebrew and means:

1. a crowd (especially of soldiers): — army, band (of men), company, troop (of robbers)
2. marauding band (engaged in raiding for plunder, especially roaming about and ravaging an area, to roam or go around in quest of plunder; make a raid for booty)
3. raiding band, foray (a quick, sudden attack)

Run is *rûṣ* in the Hebrew and means:

1. to run (for whatever reason, especially to rush)
2. break down, divide speedily, footman, guard, bring hastily
3. (make) run (away, through), post, to run swiftly, dart

When we leap we are springing - jumping high enough to overcome an obstacle. When we leap we are demonstrating that we have risen above an obstacle. We are asserting authority over that obstacle and displaying that it has no power to hinder us. We have conquering authority, rank, power, etc., so as to govern, control, or have jurisdiction regarding that obstacle.

When we leap we have to eventually land. When we land we are in a new place. This is indeed a new place of conquering and sense walls do not move, the only way we can get back behind it again is to go backwards, get behind it and allow it to seize us in again.

Decreeing you leap over walls and continue to go forward in advancing and living out your breakthrough. #SHIFT

Becoming A Storehouse Of Weapons

Even as you are God's weapon, ask God for spiritual weapons to annihilate the enemy as your weapons are not carnal but mighty and spiritual to annihilate and overthrow strongholds (2Corinthians 10:4-5).

- ***Jeremiah 50:25 New Living Bible:*** *The LORD has opened his armory and brought out weapons to vent his fury. The terror that falls upon the Babylonians (my regions and sphere of influence) will be the work of the Sovereign LORD of Heaven's Armies.*

  King James Bible: *The LORD hath opened his armoury, and hath brought forth the weapons of his indignation: for this is the work of the Lord GOD of hosts in the land of the Chaldeans.*

  The Amplified Bible: *The Lord has opened His armory and has brought forth [the nations who unknowingly are] the* *weapons of His indignation and wrath, for the Lord God of hosts has work to do in the land of the Chaldeans.*

New English Bible: *I have opened up the place where my weapons are stored. I have brought out the weapons for carrying out my wrath. For I, the Lord GOD who rules over all, have work to carry out in the land of Babylonia (my region and sphere of influence).*

The Lord has opened his store house of weapons - his armory in me, through me, and unto me. The Lord has released me as his weapon of indignation and wrath against principalities, powers, territorial spirits, foot soldier demons, strongholds, and every wicked thing that has exalted against him, his kingdom, me, my region, and sphere of influence. God has made his storehouse of weapons available inside of me and to me to annihilate the enemy. I recognize that my weapons are not carnal, but mighty through God to overthrow and dismantle every stronghold and demonic power. I use the weapons from the kingdom of heaven to destroy and overthrow ALL demonic entities.

- ***Job 38:21-23*** *Hast thou entered into the treasures of the snow? or hast thou seen the treasures of the hail, Which The Lord have reserved against the time of trouble, against the day of battle and war?*

  The Message Bible: *Have you ever traveled to where snow is made, seen the vault where hail is stockpiled, the arsenals of hail and snow that I keep in readiness for times of trouble and battle and war?*

Sidebar Revelation: *In this scripture according to Strong's Concordance, "treasures" means "storehouse of armor." Snow halts, discomfits and freezes things and hail releases judgment and destruction. God is saying have you entered the storehouses* *where I prepare and make my weapons and do you even realize that I have been preparing you in my storehouses of armor for such a time as this. The dance ministers being released in this season are weapons from heaven's storehouse of armor. He has prepared instruments of death – warring glory carriers, for such a time as this.*

I am your armor of snow that halts and discomfits the enemy Lord. I am your judgement of hail that pounces to death on the enemy. I willingly enter battle and war for your glory, for I recognize that your kingdom suffers violence and I your violent warring glory carrier, take your kingdom by force.

Becoming A Weapon of Wrath

- ***Isaiah 13:5*** *They come from faraway lands, from the ends of the heavens--the LORD and the weapons of his wrath--to destroy the whole country.*

  The Amplified Bible: *They come from a distant country, from the uttermost part of the heavens [the far east] – even the Lord and the weapons of His indignation – to seize and destroy the whole land.*

Lord I come from my secret place of preparation and enter regions as a willing laborer - as a weapon of indignation and wrath - to seize and destroy wickedness and demonic entities, while possessing and transforming the land for you glory.

- ***Isaiah 13:15*** *Whoever is captured will be thrust through; all who are caught will fall by the sword.*

Lord I decree I am your sword of mass destruction that captures and thrust through to utter destruction every enemy.

The Power Of Your Shout

- ***Jeremiah 50:15*** *Shout against her on every side! She surrenders, her towers fall, her walls are torn down. Since this is the vengeance of the LORD, take vengeance on her; do to her as she has done to others.*

Shout is *rua* in the Hebrew and means, *"to mar (especially by breaking); figuratively, to split the ears (with sound), i. e. shout (for alarm or joy)."*

- ***The Amplified Bible:*** *Raise the battle cry against her round about! She gives her hand [in agreement] and surrenders; her supports and battlements fall, her walls are thrown down. For this is the vengeance of the Lord: take vengeance on her; as she has done [to others], do to her.*

  The Message Bible: *Shout battle cries from every direction. All the fight has gone out of her. Her defenses have been flattened, her walls smashed. 'Operation God' s Vengeance. Pile on the vengeance! Do to her as she has done. Give her a good dose of her own medicine!*

I decree my shout releases a vengeance against fortified demonic cities, regions, kingdoms, and strongholds. I release my shout in every direction to snuff out the strength and fight of the enemy and his fortress. I shout and the enemies' defenses are flattened - walls are smashed to utter destruction. Operation God's Vengeance! Pile on the vengeance! With my shout, I do to my enemies as they have done to me and to others, to my city, my region, my sphere of influence and nation. With my shout, I give demons and demonic kingdoms a good dose of their own medicine!

- ***Psalms 18:6-15 English Standard Bible:*** *In my distress I called upon the Lord; to my God I cried for help. From his temple he heard my voice, and my cry to him reached his* *ears. Then the earth reeled and rocked; the foundations also of the mountains trembled and quaked, because he was angry (weapons of the Lord's anger and wrath). Smoke went up from his nostrils, and devouring fire from his mouth; glowing coals flamed forth from him. He bowed the heavens and came down; thick darkness was under his feet. He rode on a cherub and flew; he came swiftly on the wings of the wind.*

He made darkness his covering, his canopy around him, thick clouds dark with water. Out of the brightness before him hailstones and coals of fire broke through his clouds. The Lord also thundered in the heavens, and the Most High uttered his voice, hailstones and coals of fire. And he sent out his arrows and scattered them; he flashed forth lightnings and routed them. Then the channels of the sea were seen, and the foundations of the world were laid bare at your rebuke, O Lord, at the blast of the breath of your nostrils.

Psalms 149:4-6 *Let the high praises of God be in their mouth, and a twoedged sword in their hand; To execute vengeance upon the heathen, and punishments upon the people; To bind their kings with chains, and their nobles with fetters of iron; To execute upon them the judgment written: this honour have all his saints. Praise ye the Lord.*

Sidebar Revelation: *"A high praise" according to this scripture causes a spiritual alarm to be released and an uprising, so our dance should be doing just that. We also should be avenging the will of God for the people, the community, and region, and asserting his judgment and justice as our movements are unveiled.*

I decree the high praises of God are in my mouth and in my movements, and a twoedged sword in my hand, and is the literal embodiment of who I am. I decree I execute vengeance upon the heathen, and punishments upon the people. I bind every demonic king with chains, and nobles with fetters of iron. I execute upon them the judgment written: this honour is for me and all God's saints. I am his saint, his servant, his friend, his laborer, his ambassador in the earth! Praise ye the Lord! Through him I prevail with honor and triumph! Praise ye the Lord!

The Power Of Words

- ***Psalms 81:10*** *I am the LORD thy God, which brought thee out of the land of Egypt: open thy mouth wide, and I will fill it*

  Psalms 119:131 *I opened my mouth, and panted: for I longed for thy commandments.*

  New International Bible *I open my mouth and pant (Hebrew word is "saap" and means eagerly desire, devour, swallow up, to crush and trample up), longing for your commands.*

  Verse 129-131 The Message Bible: *Every word you give me is a miracle word – how could I help but obey? Break open your words, let the light shine out, let ordinary people see the meaning. Mouth open and panting, I wanted your commands more than anything.*

  The Amplified Bible *Your testimonies are wonderful [far exceeding anything conceived by man]; therefore my [penitent] self keeps them [hearing, receiving, loving, and obeying them]. The entrance and unfolding of Your words give light; their unfolding gives understanding (discernment and comprehension) to the simple. I opened my mouth and panted [with eager desire], for I longed for Your commandments.*

  New English Bible says his words are a *"doorway."* Whewww!!! Your rules are marvelous. Therefore, I observe them. Your instructions are a doorway through which light shines. They give insight to the untrained. I open my mouth and pant, because I long for your commands.

Psalms 119:105 *Your words are a lamp unto my feet a light unto my path.*

I decree that as I am obedient in opening my mouth and ministering through the movement of your Holy Spirit, that you are filling me with the miraculous.

Your words and movements in me:

- ✓ Are illuminating glory light that allows others to see and be in awe of you.
- ✓ Releasing instruction, commandments, and insight to the untrained.
- ✓ Gives unfolding understanding (discernment and comprehension) to the simple.
- ✓ Are a doorway birthing forth your kingdom, will, purpose, and intent in my midst.
- ✓ Are a lamp in my feet and for my feet Jesus, lighting my every step upon your ordained path.
- ✓ Is unveiling a panting, a seek, a hunger, a vulnerability, a yearning, to worship hard after you, to live for you, to love you, to want nothing but you.

<u>Executing Judgment</u>

- ***Psalms 119:20*** *My soul breaks for the longing that it has unto your judgments at all times.*

I decree my soul is longing to be judged by you and to release your judgement at all times. I am your movement of justice in the earth as my soul breaks forth what pleases you, edifies you, and gives you glory.

- ***Psalms 149:3-9*** *Let them praise his name in the dance: let them sing praises unto him with the timbrel and harp. For the Lord taketh pleasure in his people: he will beautify the meek with salvation. Let the saints be joyful in glory: let them sing aloud upon their beds. Let the high praises of God be in their mouth, and a twoedged sword in their hand; To execute vengeance upon the heathen, and punishments upon the people; To bind their kings with chains, and their nobles with fetters of iron; To execute upon them the judgment written: this honour have all his saints. Praise ye the Lord.*

I decree I execute capital punishment on all wickedness, principalities, and powers. I murder, assassinate, put to death according to law. I recognize that these are specific assignments of releasing vengeance and judgment on enemies and wickedness. I also understand and declare that I am exacting punishment through my movements. When I exact punishment, I am bringing rebuke, reproof, correction, chastisement, and reasoning. I am expressing God's disapproval and my personal disapproval, while scolding the enemy and wickedness for their actions.

As a weapon mass destruction, I literally bind wickedness, principalities and powers as an act of imprisonment. I dismantle, displace, and demolish nobles and kings. For I am a weapon of mass destruction that makes sure the presence and impact of these principalities and ruling powers are overthrown, where they cannot defy God anymore. This is my mindset as a weapon of God.

Created To Annihilate Evil

- ***Isaiah 54:17*** *No weapon that is formed against me will prosper; And every tongue that accuses me in judgment God condemns. This is my heritage as a servants of the LORD, And my vindication is from my declaring and establishing LORD who has the only and final word for my life.*

Verse 16-17 New Living Bible: *I have created the blacksmith who fans the coals beneath the forge and makes the weapons of destruction. And I have created the armies that destroy. But in that coming day no weapon turned against you will succeed. You will silence every voice raised up to accuse you. These benefits are enjoyed by the servants of the Lord; their vindication will come from me. I, the Lord, have spoken!*

Condemn means in this passage of scriptures means to, *"judge, censure, sentence to punishment, to judge or pronounce to be unfit for use or service.*

I decree no weapon formed against me will ever prosper. Every tongue and lofty thing that rises against me in judgment is condemned and thwarted to nothing - annihilated in Jesus name. I decree you are judged, censured, sentenced to eternal damnation, and pronounced unfit for use or service in my life, lineage, region, and sphere of influence in Jesus name. This is my heritage. I claim it and assert my authority in it as God's servant, friend, daughter, queen, weapon, and destroyer in the earth.

- ***1Samuel 2:9*** *He will guard the feet of His saints, but the wicked shall be silent in darkness. For by strength no man shall prevail. The adversaries of the Lord shall be broken in pieces; from heaven He will thunder against them. The Lord will judge the ends of the earth. He will give strength to His king, and exalt the horn of His anointed.*

I decree God will guard my feet, as the wicked and their assignments are silenced in darkness. The strength of the wicked shall not prevail. The adversaries of the Lord are broken in pieces as heaven thunders and judges them. God is strengthening me even now, for he strengthens me, his kingly ambassador. He is exalting me even now. He is exalting his power and authority in me. I trample over every enemy!

- ***Luke 11:20*** *But if I with the finger of God cast out devils, no doubt the kingdom of God is come upon you.*

  Psalms 144:1 New Living Bible: *A psalm of David. Praise the LORD, who is my rock. He trains my hands for war and gives my fingers skill for battle.*

Lord, thank you for teaching my hands to war and my fingers to fight. I demolish devils and wickedness with my bare hands. I snuff out the demonic and release your kingdom through my very fingers - the fingers of God and his delivering power that infuses me.

- ***Psalms 18:29-36*** *For by you Lord, I have run through a troop; and by you God have I leaped over a wall. As for God, his way is perfect: the word of the Lord is tried: he is a buckler to all those that trust in him. For who is God save the Lord? or who is a rock save our God? It is God that girdeth me with strength, and maketh my way perfect. He maketh my feet like hinds' feet, and setteth me upon my high places. He teacheth my hands to war, so that a bow of steel is broken by mine arms. Thou hast also given me the shield of thy salvation: and thy right hand hath holden me up, and thy gentleness hath made me great. Thou hast enlarged my steps under me, that my feet did not slip.*

  Psalms 18:37 *I have pursued my enemies and overtaken them; I did not turn until they were consumed.*

  Psalms 18:38 *I have wounded them and they are not able to rise, they have fallen under my feet.*

  Psalms 18:40 *You Lord have given me the necks of my enemies and I will destroy them in the name of Jesus.*

Psalms 18:42 *I will beat my enemies small as the dust and cast them out as mire in the streets.*

Psalms 18:50 *I am your anointed and you give me great deliverance.*

Psalms 91:13 *I tread upon the lion and adder, the young lion and dragon I trample under foot.*

Luke 10:19 *I tread upon serpents and scorpions and over all the power of the enemy and nothing shall by any means hurt me.*

Malachi 4:3 *I tread down the wicked and they are ashes under the souls of my feet.*

Micah 4:13 *I will arise and thresh and beat in pieces the enemy.*

I defeat all who defy you and defy me Jesus! I am your annihilator, your destroyer, your weapon of mass destruction! SHIFT!

Chapter 6
Identifying Fivefold Dancers
By: Minister Nina Cook

> ***Ephesians 4:11-14*** *And he gave the* ***apostles****, the* ***prophets****, the* ***evangelists****, the* ***shepherds (pastors)*** *and* ***teachers****, to equip the saints for the work of ministry, for building up the body of Christ, until we all attain to the unity of the faith and of the knowledge of the Son of God, to mature manhood, to the measure of the stature of the fullness of Christ, so that we may no longer be children tossed to and fro by the waves and carried about by every wind of doctrine, by human cunning, by craftiness in deceitful schemes.*

The Apostle:

Apostle is derived from the classical Greek word "apostolos," meaning "one who is sent." The meaning of apostle translated into Latin is "missio", which means missionary. The apostle dancer tends to operate as they are sent by God and are given strategic missions from Him to advance His kingdom. Supernatural power, miracles, signs, and wonders, are a trademark of their ministry.

> ***Acts 5:12 Amplified Bible*** *At the hands of the apostles many signs and wonders (attesting miracles) were continually taking place among the people. And by common consent they all met together [at the temple] in [the covered porch called] Solomon's portico.*

> ***Acts 19:11-17 Amplified Bible*** *God was doing extraordinary and unusual miracles by the hands of Paul, so that even handkerchiefs or face-towels or aprons that had touched his skin were brought to the sick, and their diseases left them and the evil spirits came out [of them].*

God was doing extraordinary miracles through the apostle Paul that even cloth materials that he touched brought healing and deliverance to those who came in contact with them. Apostle dancers should carry the power to bring forth healing, miracles, signs, and wonders, within their very nature.

> ***Luke 9:1-3 Amplified Bible*** *Then Jesus called together the Twelve [apostles] and gave them power and authority over all demons, and to cure diseases, And He sent them out to announce and preach the kingdom of God and bring healing. And He said to them, Do not take anything for your journey- neither walking stick, nor wallet [for a collection bag], nor food of any kind, nor money, and do not have two undergarment (tunics).*

Jesus bestowed the twelve apostles with power and authority over demons and the power to cure diseases. He sent them out on a mission to bring healing and preach the kingdom of God contesting against the demonic. He told them not to take anything with them, not food, wallets, money, or clothes to take care of themselves. As they were sent by God, they were also being supported and sustained in their assignment by God alone. Apostle dancers must lean and trust solely in God to provide for their ministry. He will give them the movements, revelation, insight and power they need to be fruitful in their assignments.

> ***1 Corinthians 2:4-5 Amplified Bible*** *And my message and my preaching were not in persuasive words of wisdom [using clever rhetoric], but [they were delivered] in demonstration of the [Holy] Spirit [operating through me] and of [His] power [stirring the minds of the listeners and persuading them], so that your faith would not rest on the wisdom and rhetoric of men, but on the power of God.*

Their ministry is not found in intellectually clever movement and performance. It comes from the provision of God, and exudes from the demonstration of the Holy Spirit and power that functions through them. The apostle dancer is inclined to have direct insight, plans, and blueprints from God that map out what their assignment and purpose is each time they have a ministry assignment. They are typically agitated, frustrated, and sometimes lost if they are in an environment that has no direction, guidance, and purpose as it pertains to effective kingdom ministry. They can also be righteously angered if they are involved in ministry that has a self-agenda, and is not God focused or rooted in the fulfilling of His will, because this is the infrastructure and rock of their ministry. For them, everything is about what God is saying, doing, and willing to do. In the Amplified Version of John 22:42, Jesus says *"not my will, but yours [always] be done."* This is how the apostle feels and how they live. As they dance, their purpose is to establish and fulfill the will of God in the earth realm.

> ***Titus 1:1-3 New Living Translation*** *This letter is from Paul, a slave of God and an apostle of Jesus Christ. I have been sent to proclaim faith to those God has chosen and to teach them to know the truth that shows them how to live godly lives. This truth gives them confidence that they have eternal life, which God – who does not lie – promised them before the world began. And now at just the right time he has revealed this message, which we announce to everyone. It is by the command of God our Savior that I have been entrusted with this work for him.*

Paul, an apostle of Jesus Christ explains that as an apostle he had been sent and entrusted to proclaim the truth of God, such that people would be transformed into embodying God's holy and pure nature in their daily lives. The truth that he proclaimed drew people out of darkness and deception into the kingdom of God, trusting in the eternal life that Jesus provided for them. The apostle dancer will release the truth of the kingdom of God through their ministry and destroy demonic deceptions that would block the people from being established in the kingdom. They carry a strong warfare capacity because they are called to overthrow demonic kingdoms and institute the kingdom of God in lives, regions and entire territories. God's anointing upon them causes them to combat, boldly confront, and demolish that which is not of God while bringing in what is of him, and what he may be specifically desiring to plant within a certain region and community of people. Since the apostles' ministry has a heavy dimension of warfare, they have been endowed with a unique power and authority that is distinct to their office, which aids them in successfully executing their God ordained assignments.

> ***Luke 10:19 Amplified Bible*** *Listen carefully: I have given you authority [that you now possess] to tread on serpents and scorpions, and [the ability to exercise authority] over all the power of the enemy (Satan); and nothing will [in any way] harm you.*

As the apostle dancer moves, they are treading on and exercising authority over the demonic spirits and powers that are operating within the people, church, community, or region they are dancing in. Their strategic movements trample, crush, and squash the enemy. This dance minister is very atmospheric, so they can shift the entire culture and nature of environments such that it is stripped of demonic infestation and reconstructed to reflect the culture of God.

Acts 19:1-9 Amplified Bible *It happened that while Apollos was in Corinth, Paul went through the upper [inland] districts and came down to Ephesus, and found some disciples. He asked them, "Did you receive the Holy Spirit when you believed [in Jesus as the Christ]?" And they said, "No, we have not even heard that there is a Holy Spirit." And he asked, "Into what then were you baptized?" They said, "Into John's baptism." Paul said, "John performed a baptism of repentance, continually telling the people to believe in Him who was coming after him, that is, [to confidently accept and joyfully believe] in Jesus [the Messiah and Savior]." After hearing this, they were baptized [again, this time] in the name of the Lord Jesus. And when Paul laid his hands on them, the Holy Spirit came on them, and they began speaking in [unknown] tongues (languages) and prophesying. There were about twelve men in all.*

And he went into the synagogue and for three months spoke boldly, reasoning and arguing and persuading them about the kingdom of God. But when some were becoming hardened and disobedient [to the word of God], discrediting and speaking evil of the Way (Jesus, Christianity) before the congregation, Paul left them, taking the disciples with him, and went on holding daily discussions in the lecture hall of Tyrannus [instead of in the synagogue].

Paul entered Ephesus and there he met some believers. He asked them if they had received the Holy Spirit and when they said "no", he gave them knowledge that although the baptism of John was good, they also needed the baptism of the Holy Spirit. He baptized them and immediately they began to speak in other tongues and prophesy. He elevated and shifted them into a new dimension of God that had not yet been planted within their region. In Romans 15:20, Paul says, *"Accordingly I set a goal to preach the gospel, not where Christ's name was already known, so that I would not build on another man's foundation;"* Apostle dancers are pioneers who usually do ground work as they dance to build the foundation of the new revelation, insight, and knowledge that God gives them. They dig up and throw out the demonic, while building the kingdom of God where the demonic once claimed ruler ship.

As Paul ministered in the synagogue of Ephesus, some became hard and disobedient to the word and they discredited and spoke evil of what he has preaching. He was enduring warfare as he pioneered within the region. The devil was not happy that his demonic structures were tumbling down as the kingdom of God was being proclaimed. As the apostle dancer pioneers, they may experience demonic resistance from people and demon spirits that seek to hinder their work. But God will cover, protect, and give this minister the means to continue prospering in their mission. Paul left taking some of the disciples with him, and held daily discussions in a lecture hall. The gospel and his purpose did not cease to flourish.

> ***Galatians 4:19 Amplified Bible*** *My little children, for whom I am again in [the pains of] labor until Christ is [completely and permanently] formed within you –*

The apostle dancer will toil until Christ is formed. As they dance, their targeted intention is to see Jesus completely permeate the people and region eternally. Their ministry labors until the fullness of Christ's will has been birthed out and is in operation. When this happens, they slip to the side as Jesus and the Holy Spirit increases and takes over.

John 3:30 The Message Version *This is the assigned moment for him to move into the center, while I slip off to the sidelines.*

Apostle Taquetta Baker

Kingdom Shifters Ministries, Muncie IN

Personal Testimony of The Dancing Apostle

I do believe there are some who are called to minister in dance as praise and worshippers, and that this is a profound ministry of sacrifice, abandonment, and adoration unto the Lord. However, when I was first asked to minister in dance, I knew my purpose had a specific calling beyond this realm of ministry. My spiritual mother had dreams and visions of me praise dancing. When she would share them with me, I would laugh and resist them. I was so bound with shame from how I danced for fun in the night clubs when I was in the world, that I barely raised my hands in church. I would be on the floor dancing from the time I entered the club until it closed at 5am in the morning. Seeing myself as a dance minister was something I just could not fathom at the time. I could not imagine myself doing anything that would even insinuate bringing reproach upon the Lord. I did not want to risk such a thing so I would be in the pews shaking and consumed by praise and worship, while refusing to surrender to the liberty that was bound within me. I eventually was delivered from shame at a women's retreat. All the women were praising and celebrating the awesome testimonies that manifested from the event and I was in my seat shaking. Someone came and challenged me with their praise moves, and I accepted the duel. As I was playing around, the spirit of praise hit me and everything that had been bottled up inside of me for years, released in abandonment. I was free from that day to praise and worship God, but still had no personal vision of being a dance minister outside of what my spiritual mother would share with me.

One day the youth pastor of the church I attended at the time, approached me and asked me to teach the youth a praise dance she saw on the TBN Network. Though I had never praise danced before, and all I had was my spiritual mother's visions, I said, "*Yes but we have to seek God for our own dance, we cannot mimic someone else's work.*" Though I did not understand it at the time, something in me knew there was a specific purpose for us ministering in dance, and that we needed our own movements and dramatization to unveil what God wanted to do and speak. As I sought God for choreography, he began to reveal to me the purpose of the dance and even that I was to start a dance ministry called "Shekinah Expressions." From the beginning, I was:

- Pioneering a dance team.
- Pioneering dance ministry where it could be embraced in my church and region.
- Pioneering revelation that praise dance was not performance but ministry.
- Pioneering revelation that dance ministers can bring deliverance, healing, and breakthrough to people, ministries, communities, regions and nations.
- Pioneering how to SHIFT the church into the prophetic and apostolic words God was speaking, and advancing the vision of the church by using the themes in each season to establish God's word in the people, church and region.
- Pioneering revelation that some dancers are more than just praise and worship ministers, and that some had specific callings to displace principalities, demolish strongholds, SHIFT atmospheres, and establish the kingdom of God in the earth.

I did not know I was doing this initially, but it was in me to do, and was the beginning of what I now know as my apostolic calling. Many dance minister's love to just praise and worship, especially when the atmosphere is liberated or just to minister unto the Lord. Though I love this as well, often when I dance, it has specific purposes of God receiving glory through some deliverance, healing, establishment, miracle, sign, wonder or God's kingdom manifesting. While others are enjoying liberation and freedom, I am discerning how the liberation of the Holy Spirit can transform lives, the atmosphere, the region, and displacing and demolishing principalities and strongholds. I am discerning how God wants to judge darkness through movement and through his presence, while establishing his kingdom in our midst. This is not intentional, it is just who I am. I have had to learn to be at peace that this is how God operates through me and how he gets glory through me. And though I can teach and impart this revelation, it is okay that others may not understand my calling, do not have this calling, or operate in this continually as their calling.

I have learned that this is the workings of the apostolic mantle upon me and that dance is one of the many ways God uses me to tear down, to displace, to overthrow, to plant, to plow, to build up, to equip.

> ***Jeremiah 1:10*** *See, I have this day set thee over the nations and over the kingdoms, to root out, and to pull down, and to destroy, and to throw down, to build, and to plant.*

In my experience, I have found that when an apostle ministers in dance, there is generally an assignment that must be completed before they can enter the realm of praising and worshipping God with pure enjoyment. Sometimes the apostle knows the assignment ahead of time, sometimes it is downloaded when they enter a sphere or event, and sometimes they are unaware what they are to combat or are combating, but their very presence has ignited controversy or war against the enemy. In order to see God's kingdom advanced in that moment, they must annihilate the enemy. I would contend that a few scriptures are everyday truths for apostles:

> ***Joshua 1:3*** *Every place that the sole of your foot shall tread upon, that have I given unto you, as I said unto Moses.*
>
> ***Psalms 108:13*** *Through God we shall do valiantly: for he it is that shall tread down our enemies.*
>
> ***Matthew 10:8*** *Heal the sick, cleanse the lepers, raise the dead, cast out devils: freely ye have received, freely give.*
>
> ***Luke 10:19*** *Behold, I give unto you power to tread on serpents and scorpions, and over all the power of the enemy: and nothing shall by any means hurt you.*
>
> ***Acts 5:12*** *And by the hands of the apostles were many signs and wonders wrought among the people; (and they were all with one accord in Solomon's porch.*

Apostles have an appetite and a drive not to share space with wickedness. They find it difficult to hang out or minister in a service where there is mixture and where people are blind to the demonic workings occurring in their midst. They find it difficult to see people bound and remain silent, while acting like God is getting glory, when his glory comes from people being saved and set free. Many apostles find this difficult at home, in the community, in their town - region, on their jobs, etc. Their very presentation and the fact that they simply walked onto - treaded upon a land - entered an atmosphere -

creates a stirring that enrages demons. The apostle is also stirred by the righteous justice brooding within them. They are compelled to produce the kingdom of God at the expense of persecution and death. As to an apostle, the kingdom of God is always at hand, and it is their lifestyle to reveal God, declare God, establish God, by any means necessary.

> ***Romans 8:36*** *As it is written, For thy sake we are killed all the day long; we are accounted as sheep for the slaughter.*
>
> ***Philippians 3:7-8*** *But whatever was an asset to me, I count as loss for the sake of Christ. More than that, I count all things as loss compared to the surpassing excellence of knowing Christ Jesus my Lord, for whom I have lost all things. I consider them rubbish, that I may gain Christ.*
>
> ***Matthew 11:12*** *And from the days of John the Baptist until now the kingdom of heaven suffereth violence, and the violent take it by force.*
>
> ***Mark 1:5*** *And saying, The time is fulfilled, and the kingdom of God is at hand: repent ye, and believe the gospel.*
>
> ***Luke 11:20*** *But if I with the finger of God cast out devils, no doubt the kingdom of God is come upon you.*

This is the reason many dancing apostles are found watching on the sidelines at many gatherings. We are:

- ✓ Discerning what principalities are at work, what strongholds are in the region and in the people, and what weapons and movements need to be used to overthrow the enemy.

- ✓ Discerning SHIFTS in the spirit realm where an opportune time is being presented to annihilate strongholds and displace principalities.
- ✓ Discerning whether God even wants to work as though we recognize a need for deliverance and breakthrough, the people of that region must be ready to sustain what God does, otherwise the enemy will return with a vengeance and stronghold them worse than before.

If we are already dancing, it is usually not for the reasons everyone else is dancing. We may even be doing the same movements, but our motives and focus is generally different and tailored to the download God is giving us. And there are instances where God will have us do movements in our seats or in the isles where we are demolishing darkness and creating a portal for his kingdom to invade.

Sometimes I feel like God is literally overtaking my body and moving through me when I am dancing. Many people speak of the power, authority, and precision they see in my movement, and how sometimes it appears as if I am dancing from another sphere. I usually have no words of explaining this as during these instances, it is as if the embodiment of God, his word, his presence, his purpose, his indignation has infused and swelled me.

An apostle's movements are usually strategic and keen. Even their turns, leaps, plies, releves, stage presence, stage direction, movement counts, movement repetitions, jabs, pointed toes, daggers hands, body contortions, choreographed or impromptu movement, etc., are significant in SHIFTING the atmosphere, displacing and annihilating darkness, opening the heavens, and bring God's kingdom to earth. Often an apostle appears to be working more than dancing. Their movements embody the very word, purpose, heart, character, and existence of God, such that the apostle know judgment, justice, decreeing, declaration, warfare, intercession, deliverance, healing, breakthrough, and wonders are occurring, even though they may not understand or be able to identify exactly what is happening through them. The dancing apostle is literally enthroned in the whole armor of God, while operating as God's holy principality. God is standing up inside the apostle of movement and establishing his Lordship and truth for all to behold, be governed by, and live through.

> **Ephesians 6:12-13** *For we wrestle not against flesh and blood, but against principalities, against powers, against the rulers of the darkness of this world, against spiritual wickedness in high places. Wherefore take unto you the whole armour of God, that ye may be able to withstand in the evil day, and having done all, to stand.*

Because of the armored mantle of God upon the dancing apostle, they are either loved or hated. They are misunderstood or accepted for their peculiarity. They are received or dreadfully rejected. The mantle upon them demands holiness and the excellency of God. You probably have heard it called "apostolic order." Apostles are ordained to bring the alignment of God to anything that is misaligned. It is an innate quality and aura radiating from them. They are not trying to judge disorder and unholiness, the God in them automatically judges disorder and unholiness. Therefore, when they walk in a room, even before they dance one movement, judgment begins. Many people are intimidated by this. Many will often shun or avoid the apostle because they feel threatened by what is automatically bringing awareness and conviction to the misalignment that is within them. Apostles usually must approach people and demonstrate the love and compassion of God, so that people will relax and embrace the fullness of who they are, and not reject them because of the Godly mantle that is upon them that they have no control over. Apostles must be okay that this is a part of their identity and influence or insecurity will cause them to abuse their authority where they come across as critical and emotionally judgmental, as opposed to operating through the confidence of healthy discernment and divine justice. When combining this with dance, an apostle pioneering a ministry that is still being embraced in the body of Christ can find themselves enduring continual persecution. Not being content in one's identity can increase the warfare as the enemy will use the ignorance and religious mindsets of people to distract, dismantle, and disempower the work and vision God has granted to the apostle's hands. An insecure, broken or confused identity will have the apostle wavering, doubting God, angry and resentful, as they strive to do what God says do, and navigate through the treasons of those the apostle will minister and impart into through their dance ministry. This is because the apostle is teaching them to embrace dance ministry, teaching them the power of dance ministry, teaching them the workings of dance ministry, changing their mindset about dance and ministry as a whole, while also respecting that it takes time to plant, plow, and transform people's mindsets to embrace all of God and not just the part they understand or deem valuable. God will require the apostle to have grace and compassion for them regardless to how they reject, neglect, and dishonor the apostle. Please understand that this is a part of one's journey as an apostle, and that their actions will hurt. Despite what the apostle will endure, the person will have to still give them all God is requiring through the apostolic calling that is upon their life. A healthy identify will allow the apostle to remain focused and grounded as they trail blaze, plant, plow, and build for God's glory.

Though many apostles flow in and out of different giftings, and have times of operating as a teacher, pastor, prophet, evangelist, we all have a specific apostolic well we minister through. I minister through the well of deliverance, healing, warfare and worship. I have a friend who is a dancing apostle and she ministers through the well of teaching and equipping. When she ministers in dance, her ministry literally breaks people free as they are enlightened and taught by the word that is being unveiled through her movement. When I minister, it is evident that deliverance and healing is manifesting, as I am warring for the breakthrough of the land, people, atmosphere and/or region. I am also able to demonstrate, lead, and establish God's kingdom through abandoned warfare and worship. It is essential as an apostle that they seek God for what well their mantle flows through, as otherwise their ministry of dance can come across as wild and confusing. This is because we are able to flow like a chameleon. It feels at times, as if God pushes a button upon our mantle and we SHIFT in and out of different giftings, but knowing our well gives us keen authority. Apostles need to know their authority so they can tower over the demonic forces that will contend against them as they minister in dance, in other areas of ministry and life in general. When apostles do not know their authority, demonic forces and religious people use this as an opportunity to snuff out the work of God. Their dance can be a blessing, but they lack the power and definition to bring the full word of God to pass. People will also find it difficult to grasp what the apostle is ministering because if the apostle is not clear regarding their authority, then neither will others be clear regarding it. This can cause lots of confusion for a dancing apostle, as many will use the identity challenges to discredit the ministry of dance and make is seem demonic, insignificant, and not God's will for the kingdom. Often our wells are revealed through the dimension of ministry that manifest the strongest in our lives. Usually, God teaches the dimensions of ministry first, then over time he reveals the mantle of apostleship. The person will sometimes be used in various other office positions such as prophet, teacher, evangelist, pastor, before they realize they are an apostle. The person's authority is being solidified and is increasing during these seasons, as they learn the value and operation of the other offices and how they work with and empower the apostle. If the apostle is insecure in these seasons, it will be interwoven in their identity as an apostle. In order to dance in true apostolic authority, the apostle must first be healed in their identity. Healing will purify the apostle's identity and bring clarity to their well of apostolic authority.

As an apostle grows in their calling, they will be able to identify with other apostles, however, it will take a daily walk with God to unveil the full vision and pattern of who they are in the earth. There will be parts of the apostle's calling that are strategic to who they are and they will not find a pattern of it in the earth. A relationship with the Holy Spirit will enable the apostle to maneuver efficiently and successfully through seasons of uncertainty, persecution, and development. This will be key in growing in the precision, grace and authority as a dancing apostle and in the fullness of one's apostolic calling. As the person grows as an apostle, they will be more effective and demonstrative with signs following as a dancing apostle.

For more revelation on this subject and my testimony as an apostle please read my book entitled, "*The Apostolic Mantle: Foundational Truths On How To Wear Your Calling.*"

Other Suggested Readings:

- ✓ Spurned Into Apostleship by Jackie Green
- ✓ Apostolic Authority Deluxe Edition by Roderick L. Evans
- ✓ 50 Truths Concerning Apostolic Ministry by John Eckhardt
- ✓ Moving in the Apostolic by John Eckhardt
- ✓ Apostolic Pioneering by Stephen Garner

The Prophet:

> ***2 Kings 17:13 New Living Translation*** *Again and again the Lord had sent his prophets and seers to warn both Israel and Judah: "Turn from all your evil ways. Obey my commands and decrees – the entire law that I commanded your ancestors to obey, and that I gave you through my servants the prophets."*

Prophets in the Strong's Concordance means:

1. Inspired man
2. Spokesman
3. Speaker

Seer in the Strong's Concordance means:

1. A beholder in vision
2. Stargazer
3. Prophet
4. Vision

> ***Deuteronomy 18:18 English Standard Version*** *I will raise up for them a prophet like you from among their brothers. And I will put my words in his mouth, and he shall speak to them all that I command him.*

Prophet dancers are inspired spokesman and visionaries of God who release the commands of the Lord. Whether the people or regions receive, align, and grasp the revelation being released, the prophet dancer must fearlessly dance what God is showing or speaking to them (Exodus 4:12). God puts his word in them and through their bodies, they release what is on the heart and mind of God for the people, regions and territories they minister in. Prophetic dance ministry is not about going before the people and free styling. The true dance of a prophet is about being connected to God and ministering from a place of revelation and conveyed knowledge. Prophetic dance is movement inspired by what is seen and heard from God within the realm of the spirit. They operate from what they see God doing, and bring what they see in the spirit into natural manifestation. They desire to see a turning and surrendering to the laws and decrees of God.

> ***Revelation 1:10-11 New American Bible*** *I was caught up in spirit on the Lord's day and heard behind me a voice as loud as a trumpet, which said, "Write on a scroll what you see and send it to the seven churches: to Ephesus, Smyrna, Pergamum, Thyatira, Sardis, Philadelphia, and Laodicea."*

As they dance, many times they are caught up in the spirit as God speaks to them and gives them vision concerning what they are to minister. It is one thing for a prophet dancer to ascend into the heavenly places at any moment, but it is a whole other thing for that minister to be able to translate what they see in heaven into the earth. The prophet dancer must be able to bring heaven to earth or a dimension of their ministry will be missing. Their heavenly visitations will be a blessing to them, but not minister to others. Through movement, they can write upon the people, atmosphere, and region what they see and can release entire prophetic words without saying one word. There is a member of my arts production company who is a prophet dance minister, she is also a prophet in training. When she steps forward to lead as we dance praise and worship, her eyes immediately shift to gazing and peering into the spirit realm. Because she knows who she is, she rapidly steps into this position. We can tell when she has been caught up in the heavenly places, when she is judging disobedience and rebellion to the commands of God, and when she is bringing the revelation she has received from heaven into the earth. We used to have to tell her to come back to make sure she did not get wrapped up in the heavens, while forgetting about the rooting and grounding of the word and ministry God was releasing in that moment. Now she can minister as both a heavenly and earthly spokesman of God.

The prophet dancer must always be seeking the Lord as they dance so they do not miss what God is doing and saying, and as a result, cause others to miss out as well. Amos 3:7 New Living Translation *says "Indeed, the Sovereign Lord never does anything until he reveals his plans to his servants the prophets."* God has secret counsel and conversation with his prophet ministers, which is why it is important for them to stay in tune with God and His spirit. Since only God could communicate these secrets to them, they bring healing and deliverance to people's lives. People are blessed by the prophet dancer, but can sometimes be taken aback or resistant because they know things only God would know. While dancing, they utilize their sight in the spirit realm and revealed secrets from God to minister specific strategic movements that bring immense transformation to all who receive of them. For example, they may minister movements around a person that demonstrate breaking and destroying demonic bondages of depression and witchcraft over their life, or they may hug and sway from side to side with a person to fill them with the love and healing presence of God.

Jeremiah 7:21-28 English Standard Version *Thus says the Lord of hosts, the God of Israel: "Add your burnt offerings to your sacrifices, and eat the flesh. For in the day that I brought them out of the land of Egypt, I did not speak to your fathers or command them concerning burnt offerings and sacrifices. But this command I gave them: 'Obey my voice, and I will be your God, and you shall be my people. And walk in all the way that I command you, that it may be well with you.' But they did not obey or incline their ear, but walked in their own counsels and the stubbornness of their evil hearts, and went backward and not forward.*

From the day that your fathers came out of the land of Egypt to this day, I have persistently sent all my servants the prophets to them, day after day. Yet they did not listen to me or incline their ear, but stiffened their neck. They did worse than their fathers. "So you shall speak all these words to them, but they will not listen to you. You shall call to them, but they will not answer you. And you shall say to them, 'This is the nation that did not obey the voice of the Lord their God, and did not accept discipline; truth has perished; it is cut off from their lips.

Acts 7:52 English Standard Version *Which of the prophets did your fathers not persecute? And they killed those who announced beforehand the coming of the Righteous One, whom you have now betrayed and murdered,*

They encounter warfare from people and regions because the word their dance embodies demands a surrendering and aligning to the commands of God. Their dance commands deliverance and change, which causes them to press against those who are not willing to change, and demonic powers that have locked regions and people, thus inhibiting them from change. They can heed warnings and earnestly caution the people to regard the word of the Lord. God may tell them to minister movements of judgement upon people, demons, and regions, if there has been no repentance regarding his previous warnings and commands.

> **2 Peter 1:21 English Standard Version** *For no prophecy was ever produced by the will of man, but men spoke from God as they were carried along by the Holy Spirit.*
>
> ***Jeremiah 1:9 English Standard Version*** *Then the Lord put out his hand and touched my mouth. And the Lord said to me, "Behold, I have put my words in your mouth.*

Their dance comes directly from what God has deposited in them. It does not come from the will of man or their personal desires. They do not minister to appease or please the people. When God anoints and fills them, they release what thus saith Lord.

Minister Reenita Keys
Manifold Grace Production Company Muncie, IN
Personal Testimony of the Prophet Dancer

It has been a pleasure to articulate the prophetic word of the Lord through movement. As an emerging prophet and minister of dance, the process caused me to shift further into destiny alignment. Becoming a minister of dance has challenged, pressed, pushed, and caused every boundary and barrier within me, to stretch beyond the natural limits I set for myself. Before accepting the call to dance with Manifold Grace Production Company, I did not have experience or training. I had an idea who I was, nor did I know I was called to dance. There were countless hours spent dancing in my college dorm room in secret, while running from the call to dance. I had a heart that wanted to bellow the rivers of worship upon the Lord. During this time, it was the beginning stages of my walk with the Lord, where I began to learn more about the five-fold offices, spiritual warfare, the spirit realm, and dimensions of the prophetic. While dancing, I would have heavenly encounters with the Lord. I would find myself wrapped up in holy places that words cannot fathom or explain. The Lord would cause my worship to translate me into the secret places of His heart and I had open access to roam the heavens. Through the art of worship, I accessed prophetic words, activations, and realms of decreeing a thing from heaven into the earth. I found myself dancing my way through warfare and breaking regional strongholds with strategy and precision. Prophetic worship was a part of my life although this was only the beginning.

Manifold Grace Production Company further equipped me with the very knowledge that was needed to shift from gifting to calling, while cultivating the art and gift of dance that needed to be further activated and unleashed from within me. There were many teachings, tools, and hands-on demonstrations to stretch the very thing that was already inside of me. My dance leader, Nina Cook, knocked down many misperceptions, glass-ceilings, and stereotypes about dance. She trained her team as Navy Seals who knew they were being sent into regions and territories as an apostle, prophet, preacher, teacher, or evangelist and not as traditional dancers. Nina has always been one of great faith and did not care if you have never taken a dance class in your life. If the Lord revealed a dance move that required technical skill and years of training, she did not box her team in. She activated them in the movements immediately regardless of their technique and dance skill level. She would teach the dance move and cause every eagle in the nest to soar in that very move with grace, precision and excellence.

Training as a minister of dance goes beyond getting up in front of the congregation every Sunday. There are strategies of fasting, praying, deliverance, healing, intimate time spent with the Lord, growing in your walk with God, vulnerability, team building and seeking deep transformation daily, to be equipped minister to the people effectively. As a prophetic minister of dance, the Lord will show me the demonic powers, strongholds, rulers of darkness, and principalities strong holding the lives of the people and region. The Lord will also take me to the heavenly places to bring the very things the people need from the Lord to receive breakthrough. Prophetic dance causes God's character, nature, heart, and presence to establish in the people, region and atmosphere. It will cause heaven to unlock inside of a place for miracles, healing, deliverance, and breakthrough to be accessible to the people. The more I matured as a prophetic dance minister, the more I knew how to draw people into the supernatural power of God. As I continue to journey as a prophetic dancer, I have a burning desire to mirror the movement of heaven on earth, establish the word of the Lord, and uproot evil powers of darkness. I want people to come into the full vision of the Lord for their lives, not just a measure. Manifold Grace Production Company allows me to produce the word and heavenly mysteries of God with every assignment that is released. I decree the Lord will continue to raise up prophetic dance ministers around the world with purity and strength to come out of the secret places and shift from gifting to calling.

Minister Kim Bacon
Soar Prophetic Ministries Minneapolis, MN

The Prophet who happens to dance is an artistic expression of the Power of God in motion. Prophets are spokesmen for the Almighty God. They only speak and communicate what the Father God tells them to say. Prophetic dancers are divine portals for the supernatural to flow in the midst of His people. As we know, every word that precedes from the mouth of God is potent, purposeful, and will not return void of demonstration. It is the same with the Prophet who ministers through dance. Our bodies are embodied decrees. Decrees establish laws and enforce the laws. Keep in mind, when a king makes a decree it cannot be altered or stopped, it must be done. Every movement released by a prophet dancer is precise, strategic and intentional. We are wise master builders and birth the miraculous with every spin, clap, stomp, look and prophetic act.

A Prophet dancer must be sensitive to the timing of God and the divine drive of heaven. I recall being at a worship service and the minstrels began to flow prophetically. I heard the Holy Spirit clearly say to me get the white veil and minster with it because He wanted to release His life given breath in the atmosphere and blow over specific ones. As I obeyed, the Holy Spirit gave me the movement and the people He wanted to breathe on and resuscitate with His breath. Each release was different and tailor made for the soul the Holy Spirit wanted to touch. I put the white veil over the head of one lady and she cried like a newborn baby. The Holy Spirit had me to wrap the veil around another lady's shoulders and she fell to her knees repenting for doubting him, and the last lady the Holy Spirit literally used the veil as a fresh wind and she fell out from His presence. The Holy Spirit took over the worship service and released life. I am not saying this as if I did something so great. I am telling you this because as prophets we belong to God. Anytime He wants to speak, we must be ready to proclaim. I want to share another way the Holy Spirit uses the prophet dancer. It is through strategic choreography. I was asked to choreograph a ministry piece for a dance worship service. After prayer, the Holy Spirit gave me "Healing" by Richard Smallwood. He shared with me that most people are bound and ill because of the negative words they speak. In the beginning of the piece, there was a 1 minute dramatization where a dancer would speak something negative and a demon would put chains around her. Before the song came on she was so bound she could not move. In the choreography, there were certain movements to words that he sung such as "there's a balm in Gilead to heal your soul." The dancer would lift up the chains every time she would hear those words. She became free and began ministering with the other dancers. Well I did not know, but God knew there was a lady in the auditorium that said if God did not speak to her that night she was going to kill herself when she left the dance worship service. She said that the Holy Spirit flashed her life before her after the ministry piece. He spoke to her that she was in the state she was in because her own negative words had snared her. Praise God, through prophetic choreography a soul was saved. We must grasp who we are to the King and in this kingdom. We must come to a resolute that we carry weight in the spirit as prophetic movers. Do not lose sight of your mandate as a prophet dancer, you are a powerhouse demonstrator.

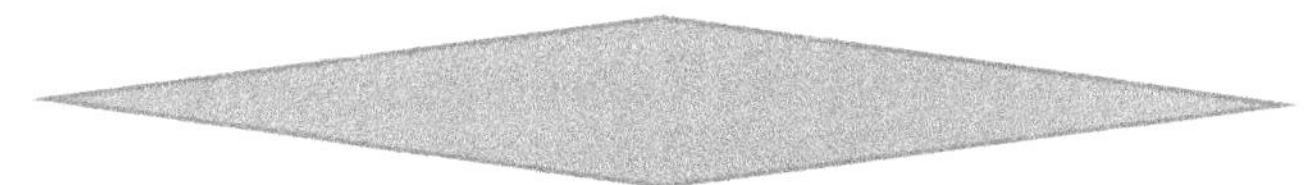

The Evangelist:
Evangelist in the Greek is euangelos. Eu means "good" and "angelos" (nearly always translated angel").

It means "messenger"- one who is sent in order to announce, teach, or perform a thing.

- They proclaim a good message, or good news.
- They preach the Gospel, bring good tidings, show glad tidings, as it pertains to the gospel.
- They bring people into relationship with the message of salvation- which is Jesus Christ.

Evangelist dancers bring a manifestation of Jesus and his saving drawing power through their ministry. They always carry a message within and have a heart for the people to connect and come into relationship with Christ. They bring good tidings, show glad tidings, and minister the gospel as they dance. Releasing the love, joy, salvation, redemption, and message of Jesus Christ. Their ministry always ties back to Jesus, who He is to us, what he did for us, and what He has made available for us. Although there is great joy released through the ministry of the evangelist, it is not always about expressing the joy of the Lord. It will also display lowliness, brokenness, hurt, and woundedness, in order to relate to people's situations, cause them to be pricked to look at themselves and their current situations, and see why they need Jesus in their lives. They will easily show a depiction of the people, and the people will be able to connect because they feel like "oh that's me." They will feel like the dancer is telling their story because of how relatable it is and how the evangelist dance minister has interjected their lives and situations. Because the people receive of the ministry as if it was their own life, they are being transformed as the minister dances out a clear distinct picture of themselves, and what they are going through. It is like Jesus taking their burdens and lifting things off of them, as the dance ministers healing, deliverance and cleansing, setting them free of their challenges.

> **1 Peter 5:7** *Casting all your care upon him; for he careth for you.*

> **Psalms 55:22** *Cast thy burden upon the LORD, and he shall sustain thee: he shall never suffer the righteous to be moved.*

The evangelist dance minister desires for the people to be saved, come into the knowledge of Jesus, and the truth that he is the one and only God who has the power to save them.

> **1 Timothy 2:4-5** *Who will have all men to be saved, and to come unto the knowledge of the truth. For there is one God, and one mediator between God and men, the man Christ Jesus;*

Although the minister may display brokenness, hurt, or whatever the situation of the people may be, they do not stay in this place. As they dance they will shift into showing how the power of Jesus, the gospel, and the message they are proclaiming brings transformation, healing, miracles, and deliverance into their lives, churches, communities, and regions.

> **Romans 1:16** *New Living Translation For I am not ashamed of this Good News about Christ. It is the power of God at work, saving everyone who believes – the Jew first and also the Gentile.*

Power in the Strong's Concordance in this scripture means:

1. Force
2. Miraculous power, a miracle itself, ability, abundance

3. Power, strength, violence, mighty (wonderful) work
4. Inherit power, power residing in a thing by virtue of its nature, or which a person or thing exerts and puts forth power for performing miracles
5. Moral power and excellence of soul
6. The power and influence which belong to riches and wealth
7. Power and resources arising from numbers
8. Power consisting in or resisting in or resting upon armies, forces, hosts

The power for miracles, strength, influence, and heavenly resources is released through the message of Jesus that they carry.

Evangelism is a soul winning ministry, therefore it goes to war with the darkness set against the souls of the people. Often, we are taught that the evangelist ministry is about drawing people and bringing them to church. But there is war on this ministry because after drawing the people, the demonic bondages upon their souls must be dealt with to help them sustain in the Lord, and truly see their lives transformed. As an evangelist dancer, you draw the people, but you also go to war for their soul.

In Greek literature, evangelizo was also used of liberation from enemies as well as deliverance from demonic power. As the evangelist dance minister goes forth, they deliver and liberate people from the bondages of sin and demonic powers that have claim over them. They transfer lives from the ownership of darkness into the ownership of light. They aim to gain dominion of your soul for the kingdom of God.

> **1 Peter 2:9** *But ye are a chosen generation, a royal priesthood, an holy nation, a peculiar people; that ye*

should shew forth the praises of him who hath called you out of darkness into his marvellous light:

Minister Mercedes Carr
Manifold Grace Production Company Muncie, IN
Personal Testimony of the Evangelist Dancer

My process to becoming a minister of dance has been everything but simple. It has been a very dynamic, exciting, yet challenging experience accepting the fullness of my calling, purpose, and destiny not only as a dance minister, but as a minister in general. Manifold Grace Production company was not my first experience in dance, but it was my first experience ministering in dance with an understanding of the tools, weapons, and strategies that ministers of dance hold through the Holy Spirit. As one who has been a part of praise dance ministry since the age of 9, I would have considered myself pretty knowledgeable about dance ministry, but those experiences only scratched the surface to my life as a dance minister. The moment I joined Manifold Grace I was not only equipped as a dancer but as an evangelist, a 5-Fold minister, and a woman of God. My dance leader stretched me in many ways that caused me to shift into the fullness of my destiny and purpose, and she has always been a firm believer of healing, deliverance, equipping, training, and releasing you to be the whole person that God ordained you to be through love. Becoming a minister of dance in Manifold Grace was never about performing, putting on a show, or impressing the people! It was and is always about saving souls, shifting atmospheres, setting people free, and establishing Gods kingdom here on earth. Manifold Grace empowered me to explore who I was as a dance minister. It transform my dance, but also transformed my life! The tools I received allowed me to shift into walking in true purpose and destiny even when it was difficult. I learned strategies for fasting, intercession, warfare, prophetic dance, personal relationship with God, personal relationships with people, and so much more! Each of these things are incorporated and vital in my position as a minister of dance. Dance has become a lifestyle of ministry before the Lord and the more deliverance, healing and freedom I receive in my personal relationship with the Father the more effective, liberated and anointed my dance becomes! Dance ministry without healing, deliverance, and submission to the Lord first will always be void of Gods true power, healing, deliverance, conversion and transformation!

When dancing as an evangelistic minister, I can see the needs of the people before me. I can often feel their pain, joy, sorrow, as well as whatever they are needing at the time. The Lord uses my movement to pluck out, wash, cleanse, impart, and connect the people with the heart of God for their lives and it is very liberating! As an evangelist, my call is to proclaim the good news and preach the unadulterated gospel of Jesus Christ to bring people into the Kingdom of God. Through my dancing, it is my vision to bring believers and non-believers into a place of repentance and even conversion to truly shift them into seeking the truth of Gods plan and desires for their salvation and lives. I have to stay in a place of wholeness, obedience, repentance, and filling up with Gods word and plan in order to effectively fulfill this call in life as an evangelizing minister.

Evangelistic dance brings a spirit of repentance, conviction, and a pricking of the heart to judge every ungodly place in our lives while shifting us into eliciting change and obedience to the entire plan of God for our lives. It can also bring joy, peace, comfort, support, redemption, freedom, and the love of God as he never wants to empty the people without filling them back up. As I grow, my dancing pulls and draws people out of darkness into God's marvelous light. I am very passionate about the hearts and souls of the people because I know where Gods Manifold Grace and mercy has brought me, and it is an honor to now use my gifts, anointing, power, and body, for his glory through dance and as a minister in general. I pray that my evangelistic ministry always points back to Jesus as Lord and the only way, and that my dance exudes the fullness of Isaiah 45:22 which reads *"Turn to Me and be saved, all you ends of the earth; for I am God, and there is no other" (Isaiah 45:22, NIV).*

The Pastor:

Pastor in the Strong's Concordance means:

1. A shepherd
2. A herdsman
3. In the parable, he to whose care and control others have committed themselves, and whose precepts they follow
4. Of the overseers of the Christian assemblies
5. The task of the Near Eastern shepherd were; to watch for enemies trying to attack the sheep- to defend the sheep from attackers- to heal the wounded and sick sheep- to find and save lost or trapped sheep- to love them, sharing their lives and so earning their trust

Shepherd in dictionary.com:

1. A person who herds, tends, and guards sheep
2. A person who protects, guides, or watches over a pe rson or group of people

A person who dances through a pastoral anointing is one who shepherds, oversees, cares for and seeks to protect those who they minister too. The focus of their ministry is to provide guidance and wise direction that will aid the people in following the Lord. They display what to do and what not to do through the message and movements they minister to, while advising the people in making godly decisions.

Pastoring dancers are shepherding dancers. Their ministry aims to protect people from the deceptions and demonic operations that would intend to harm their lives and draw them away from Christ. They embody and exude the heart and love of God through their ministry. They are very people oriented and there is a level of personal connection and intimacy they desire to have with the people as they minister. They want to speak a direct message that will provide leadership, guidance, direction, advice and care that will not only bless the people, but cause them to follow after what God is speaking through them.

> ***Acts 20:28-29 Amplified Bible*** *Take care and be on guard for yourselves and for the whole flock over which the Holy Spirit has appointed you as overseers, to shepherd (tend, feed, guide) the church of God which He bought with His own blood. I know that after I am gone, [false teachers like] ferocious wolves will come in among you, not sparing the flock;*
>
> ***Isaiah 40:11 Amplified Bible*** *He will protect His flock like a shepherd, He will gather the lambs in His arm, He will carry them in His bosom; He will gently and carefully lead those nursing their young.*

As they dance, they are nurturing and cultivating within the people the message they are releasing. The shepherding grace is embedded within their movements and within the purpose of their ministry. They may use dramatizations, props and storylines to bring the fullness of their message across and provide the people with a visual display of God's word and will for them.

> ***Ezekiel 34:11-16 Amplified Bible*** *For thus says the Lord God, "Behold, I Myself will search for My flock and seek them out. As a shepherd cares for his sheep on the day that he is among his scattered flock, so I will care for My sheep; and I will rescue them from all the places to which they were scattered on a cloudy and gloomy day. I will bring them out from the nations and gather them from the countries and bring them to their own land; and I will feed them on the mountains of Israel, by the streams, and in all the inhabited places of the land. I will feed them in a good pasture, and their grazing ground will be on the mountain heights of Israel. There they will lie down on good grazing ground and feed in rich pasture on the mountains of Israel. I will feed My flock and I will let them lie down [to rest]," says the Lord God. "I will seek the lost, bring back the scattered, bandage the crippled, and strengthen the weak and the sick; but I will destroy the fat and the strong [who have become hard-hearted and perverse]. I will feed them with judgment and punishment.*

> ***Luke 15:3-7 Amplified Bible*** *So He told them this parable: "What man among you, if he has a hundred sheep and loses one of them, does not leave the ninety-nine in the wilderness and go after the one which is lost, [searching] until he finds it? And when he has found it, he lays it on his shoulders, rejoicing. And when he gets home, he calls together his friends and his neighbors, saying to them, 'Rejoice with me, because I have found my lost sheep!' I tell you, in the same way there will be more joy in heaven over one sinner who*

repents than over ninety-nine righteous people who have no need of repentance.

Pastoring dancers seek and search after the people, such that they can impact the wounded, strengthen the weak, and release a message to the lost. Just like Jesus, each sheep (person) is important to them, and they feel the urgency to make them a priority.

> ***Psalms 78:70-72 Amplified Bible*** *He also chose David His servant And took him from the sheepfolds;*
> *From tending the ewes with nursing young He brought him To shepherd Jacob His people, And Israel His inheritance. So David shepherded them according to the integrity of his heart; And guided them with his skillful hands.*
>
> ***Jeremiah 3:15 Amplified Bible*** *"Then [in the final time] I will give you [spiritual] shepherds after My own heart, who will feed you with knowledge and [true] understanding.*

Pastoring dancers have the heart, integrity and ardor of God to feed and pour into the people. They are skilled specifically to provide spiritual guidance, knowledge and understanding in the ways of God.

Psalms 23:1-6 Amplified Bible
The Lord is my Shepherd [to feed, to guide and to shield me] ***Pastoring dancers minister nourishment, guidance and protection*** *I shall not want.*

He lets me lie down in green pastures; He leads me beside the still and quiet waters. ***Pastoring dancers minister safety and rest in God, peace and tranquility.***

He refreshes and restores my soul (life); He leads me in the paths of righteousness for His name's sake. ***Pastoring dancers minister life refreshing and restoration to the souls of people. Their ministry leads to paths of righteousness and godliness.***

Even though I walk through the [sunless] valley of the shadow of death, I fear no evil, for You are with me; Your rod [to protect] and Your staff [to guide], they comfort and console me. ***Pastoring dancers minster encouragement and empowerment to prevail through all seasons of life. They provide comfort, love and consolation as they dance.***

You prepare a table before me in the presence of my enemies. You have anointed and refreshed my head with oil; My cup overflows. Surely goodness and mercy and unfailing love shall follow me all the days of my life, And I shall dwell forever [throughout all my days] in the house and in the presence of the Lord. ***Pastoring dancers release fresh anointing that brings overflowing replenishment. They seek to keep the people established in God's truth, attributes and blessings that follow with having a relationship with Jesus Christ.***

Minister Ayanna S Garrett MDIV, M.Ed in Community Counseling

Living Water Community Church Bolingbrook, IL

Personal Testimony of the Pastor Dancer

"The more things change, the more they stay the same," were the first words I uttered as I stood on the stage at my church and looked at the hundreds of people in the congregation. My heart beat fast and small beads of sweat began to form across my forehead. Living in the tension of faith and being afraid, I had no idea how the congregation would receive this word. All I knew was that God called me to minster this particular word to this group of people. At that very moment, I was called to speak truth to power.

As a pastor many times we are called to speak words to people they may not want to hear, but need to hear.

It was my first time doing what I call a "dramatic sermon," or literally embodying a biblical character and preaching, dancing, acting, and even singing from their perspective. I have an arts background and began taking ballet classes at the age of 4. I had done dramatic presentations before and even preached, danced and taught throughout the United States and Europe, but there was something about my first dramatic sermon that made me tremble. You see I had the audacity to preach from Judges 19, a passage of scripture about an unnamed woman who was disrespected, devalued and abused by men. Judges 19 is what is called a difficult passage because of the brutalization of this woman. No one really wants to talk about it or the woman and preachers usually skip over the passage. I stood on the stage, began to speak and I gave the unnamed woman a voice. Although I had never seen this type of sermon done before, I knew I was mandated by God to preach it in dramatic form and to trust The Spirit of God to work on the hearts and minds of the people.

I preached a word about the value of women and how women were made in the image of God just as men and should not be disrespected, abused, or devalued. Overall, it was not a "feel good sermon" but one in which challenged people to do some head and heart work. Halfway through the sermon, people began to weep. God was working in their hearts, tearing down stereotypes and strongholds that had held them hostage for years. Towards the end of the sermon, I danced to Martha Munizzi's "I Know the Plans." As I began to dance, I embodied hope and allowed the lyrics of the song to guide my movement. I literally led the dance with my heart. As the Holy Spirit began to move through my body, I made sure my body was open so that my heart had a direct connection to heaven. I used a lot of movements with my arms outstretched to God and the people. When Ms. Munizzi began to sing the lyrics "I know the plans I have for you," I made it a point to look directly into the eyes of the people in the congregation and politely point to individuals in the congregation that God pointed out to me. With my eyes wide open and a soft smile, I ministered to the people with simple, but strong movements. As I think back to the dance, I am unsure of all the movements the dance incorporated, but I do remember incorporating numerous pique and basque turns, soft movements symbolizing God's love for us.

After the sermon, women and men alike began to come to me weeping, telling me their stories, how they experienced the sermon and thanking me for giving this woman a voice. Every time I have done a dramatic sermon, there has always been a great response from the people. God's anointing is certainly at work, but I also believe that the arts have a special way of bringing meaning and understanding to sermons that traditional preaching do not convey.

I was first introduced to dramatic sermons by my preaching professor, Dr. Ronald Allen, at Christian Theological Seminary in Indianapolis. I remember him lecturing about it and being captivated by the idea of doing a dramatic sermon. A few weeks later, I heard people at my church talking about their excitement that Easter was approaching. Yes, they were looking forward to celebrating Jesus' resurrection, but they were also in anticipation of the annual Easter dramatic sermon. Unbeknownst to me, my pastor Rev. Dr. Donald Hudson, of Umoja Christian Church in Indianapolis, was very good at dramatic sermons. I saw my first dramatic sermon that Easter. I was inspired and since then I have been writing and creating my own sermons as God gives them to me.

If you feel called to this type of ministry, I would encourage you to continue to pray, study and exegete scriptural passages just as you would for a traditional sermon. Allow the Spirit of God free reign in your creative process. If you have the resources to participate in drama, dance and/or voice workshops take advantage of the opportunities. Hone your skills as best as you can. If you are not able to afford such opportunities, ask God to send people in your life who are skilled in these areas to assist you in increasing your skills. I believe dramatic sermons should be done with excellence. You should always put your best forward and God will certainly take care of the rest. I would also encourage you to be open to the movement of the Spirit of God, whether you are in the sermon preparation process or literally in the midst of your preaching. Dramatic preaching is a non- traditional form of preaching, but a valid and effective form of preaching the gospel. If you are a little afraid to try it, I encourage you to do it afraid. With God leading you, there are no wrong moves.

The Teacher:

Teach in Dictionary.com means, *"To impart knowledge of or skill in; give instruction in."*

The Ephesians 4 mandate is to:

- Equip the saints
- Build up the body of Christ in unity and knowledge
- Bring maturity and the fullness of Christ such that God's children are no longer subject to deception by crafty demonic schemes

When a teacher dancer ministers, they are equipping and building the people in the instruction God has given them to deliver. They are imparting knowledge and skills to encourage, empower, and direct a person's journey in living a Christ-like life.

> ***Titus 2:7-8 New Living Translation*** *And you yourself must be an example to them by doing good works of every kind. Let everything you do reflect the integrity and seriousness of your teaching. Teach the truth so that your teaching can't be criticized. Then those who oppose us will be ashamed and have nothing bad to say about us.*

To be effective, the teacher dancer must apply the instruction to their own lives and be an example of the truth. As they emulate the truth, their teaching cannot be criticized. Impartation occurs because they sow the revelation they carry into others. This is why it is important for them to reflect and live by what they minister so their instructional impartation will be pure, evident and unable to be opposed. Their ministry is revelatory and contains great clarity so that those who receive can easily learn and be enlightened.

> ***1 Timothy 4:11 New Living Translation*** *Teach these things and insist that everyone learn them.*

Teach in the Strong's Concordance means:

1. To hold discourse with others in order to instruct them, deliver didactic discourses
2. Instill doctrine into one
3. The thing taught or enjoined
4. To explain or expound a thing
5. To teach one something

The teacher dancer communicates and holds conversation through their movement as if they are giving a speech. They are instilling doctrine, enjoining the message of God, and expounding it within the hearts and minds of the people. Their movements are assertive, firm and commanding as they require an aligning with the instruction God is relaying to occur.

> ***Psalm 32:8 Amplified Bible*** *I will instruct you and teach you in the way you should go; I will counsel you [who are willing to learn] with My eye upon you.*

> ***Exodus 18:20 Amplified Bible*** *You shall teach them the decrees and laws. You shall show them the way they are to live and the work they are to do.*

> ***1 Thessalonians 4:1-2 Amplified Bible*** *Finally, believers, we ask and admonish you in the Lord Jesus, that you follow the instruction that you received from us about how you ought to walk and please God (just as you are actually doing) and that you excel even more and more [pursuing a life of purpose and living in a way that expresses gratitude to God for your salvation]. For you know what commandments and precepts we gave you by the authority of the Lord Jesus.*

Their instruction gives direction and shows the people the way they should go to follow Jesus and live in a manner that is pleasing to Him. Their dance brings encouragement and empowerment to help people progress on their course with God. They provide life lessons that people can connect with and receive a personal relatable message. When they dance, a story may be told, the movement may be strongly focused in admonishing the people in what they should do, and the song choice may be filled with words that give inspiration. The teacher dancer is not limited to teaching within itself, but they instill within people, the ability to go forth in what they are receiving. They are activators who ignite, trigger and mobilize the people in the direction of God.

Apostle Renee Gray
Restored to Purpose Ministry, Michigan

Teaching in Dictionary.com means, *"to help to learn; tell or show how; to impart knowledge of or skill in; give instruction in."* Instruct, tutor, train and educate are words with similar meaning. As a teaching dancer, all these characteristics take place in every setting; preparation/rehearsal, ministering a dance piece and mentoring each dancer. Teaching is my primary focus when meeting with dancers. My goal is to explain our purpose for ministry and answer the simple questions:

- Who are we ministering to? (children, leaders, women, entire body of Christ)
- What is our message to the people of God?
- Why is this message important?
- Where is our focus for ministry?
- Do we walk in the attributes of Christ in our lives?

When these questions are understood, we are all operating together and on one accord. John 17:20-21 in the Message Bible states, *"I'm praying not only for them but also for those who will believe in me because of them and their witness about me. The goal is for all of them to become one heart and mind".* As a teaching dancer, unity is key. Amos 3:3 in the New King James Bible states, *"Can two walk together, except they be agreed?"* When dancers do not agree, it is a visual representation of being divided, which is not an attribute of Christ. Contending for unity is vital to our ministry. The teaching dancer will offer compromise to bring all to a place of unity.

Pure joy and accomplishment is gained when I have completed an assignment from beginning to end with success. When God gives me a song that will bring healing to His people, I begin to research the scriptures and choose one that will allow the dancers to see the picture of the dance. At every preparation/rehearsal, I continue to reiterate the who, what, and why, of the ministry piece. The scripture becomes the focal point of the piece, keeping our hearts and minds on one accord with God. As we minister the piece in preparation/rehearsal, I am praying that how we expect the Spirit of God to move and flood the place happens in our time of preparing. His Word is true in preparing and on the day of ministry - He is in the midst. Matthew 18:20 states, *"For where two or three are gathered together in My name, I am there in the midst of them."* I believe God will allow His dancers to experience His presence in our preparation/rehearsal time. When the dancers are aware of His presence, they learn to minister in it. They learn to control their personal urge of dancing on their own, but stay focused on God and unity to accomplish the goal. So on the day of ministry, everyone is on one accord and the presence of God fills the place - it is glorious!!

The teaching dancer is equally interested in the lives of the dancers being examples of Christ. If our lives do not align with what we are ministering, then our ministry is non-effective. We become a hindrance to healing and deliverance taking place. Mentoring dancers to live a life true to their faith keeps the ministry growing strong. Calling each dancer on a regularly scheduled day, going out to lunch or dinner, reading and praying together, are all tools to building a mentoring relationship. 1Thessalonians 5:12-13 in the Message Bible states, *"And now, friends, we ask you to honor those leaders who work so hard for you, who have been given the responsibility of urging and guiding you along in your obedience. Overwhelm them with appreciation and love!"*

I enjoy being a teaching dancer. I love to see the end result of what God desires our relationships and ministries to be.

Instructing each dancer in how their decisions should parallel the Word of God brings forth great discussions. We discuss how the Word is still true today, how others are effected by our decisions and how we can become more like Him. Training dancers in their craft and movements that speak and interpret God's Word and presence brings enlightenment. Dance is more than movement. The movement must speak to the message that God is conveying at any given moment. To be able to discern, sense and hear the voice of God can be taught. Education is an on-going attribute in our lives and walk with God. Our desire to be more like Jesus will keep us in the mind-set of a student. God is the author of creativity. Learning how to interpret His Word through movement can be accomplished and completed in many ways. Learning to accept diversity will make our ministry well rounded. The teaching dancer is pertinent to the growth of the ministry and each dancer involved.

Chapter 7
Heavenly Choreography

By: Minister Nina Cook

> **Habakkuk 2:1-3** *I will stand upon my watch, and set me upon the tower, and will watch to see what he will say unto me, and what I shall answer when I am reproved. And the LORD answered me, and said, Write the vision, and make it plain upon tables, that he may run that readeth it. For the vision is yet for an appointed time, but at the end it shall speak, and not lie: though it tarry, wait for it; because it will surely come, it will not tarry.*

This scriptural passage provides a clear description of the choreography process. Receiving movement from the Lord is like writing a vision of the word and will of God upon the hearts and minds of people, and upon the regions and territories we minister in. It is making it plain in them that they would be able to progress in the word being released. Choreography is essentially a vision of God's word manifesting through movement.

<u>*Stand* in the Strong's Concordance means:</u>

1. To stand, remain, endure, take one's stand
2. Be in a standing attitude, present oneself, become a servant of
3. To tarry, remain, continue, abide, endure, persist, be steadfast
4. To station, set, maintain
5. To appoint, ordain, establish

To receive vision for movement from the Lord you must be correctly postured to receive from him. It is an established stance, attitude, and station that you remain in through the process. It is important that before you begin to work on choreography, you receive vision about the purpose of your ministry event. This way you can build a dance where each movement embodies that purpose and is not idle movement or a hosh posh of movement. If you truly are wanting to receive movement that serves the Lord and is not just pretty, good to look at, and hype, this stance to receive from him will cause you to be inspired by the Lord.

> ***2 Timothy 3:16*** *All scripture is given by inspiration of God, and is profitable for doctrine, for reproof, for correction, for instruction in righteousness:*

Inspiration in the Strong's Concordance in this scripture means:

1. Divinely breathed in
2. Inspired by God

Inspire from Dictionary.com means:

1. To fill with an animating, quickening, or exalting influence
2. To produce or arouse (a feeling, thought, etc.)
3. To fill or affect with a specified feeling, thought, etc.
4. To influence or impel
5. To communicate or suggest by a divine or supernatural influence
6. To guide or control by divine influence
7. To prompt or instigate by influence
8. To give rise to, bring about, cause, etc.

Choreography should be divinely breathed in by God. His exalting supernatural influence should be guiding, controlling, communicating, and producing his movement in us. Just as all scripture was given by the inspiration of God, as dance ministers, our choreography which is essentially our scripture, should be received by the inspiration of God.

Cultures who serve idol gods summon their gods which are demonic spirits to receive their inspiration. Kathak is an Indian classical dance inspired by the stories of the Hindu god Krishna.

Kalilambe is an African dance symbolic of the celebration of harvest, life, and the birth of children. It is a ritual performed that worships fertility. Krump dance in the American culture is inspired by emotions of anger, rage, grief and loss, and release to reach a point of ecstasy. There are countless other dances around the world that are being inspired by demonic influence. It is important that dance ministers of God receive inspiration only from him and release the breath of God into the earth realm.

The scripture says that it is profitable for:

- Doctrine (instruction, teaching, learning) - Our choreography should teach, give instruction, and cause people to learn whatever God is speaking through our ministry
- Reproof (proof, conviction, evidence) - Our choreography should embody evidence and proof of God and bring conviction
- Correction (restoration to an upright or right state, improvement of life or character, reformation) - Our choreography should improve, restore, and reform the lives and characters of people
- Instruction in righteousness (education or training, chastening, nurture, cultivation of minds, morals, and increasing virtue, integrity, purity, correctness of thinking, feeling, and acting) - Our choreography should educate, train and cultivate people in godliness

The scripture ends by saying "That the man of God may be perfect, thoroughly furnished unto all good works." Our choreography should bring perfection, solidification, and do a complete work in the people and regions that we minister too.

One of the ways I position myself to receive movement from the Lord is through prayer. Prayer is a posture of wanting to speak to the Lord, as well as wanting to hear, see, and receive from him.

> ***Matthew 7:7*** *Ask, and it shall be given you; seek, and ye shall find; knock, and it shall be opened unto you:*

Ask in the Strong's Concordance in this scripture means:

1. To ask, beg, call for, crave, desire

You ask and call for God to show you his movement. Place before him your desire to receive choreography inspired by only him.

Seek in the Strong's Concordance in this scripture means:

1. To worship God, desire, endeavor, enquire for, require
2. To seek in order to find purposeful intentional direct
3. By thinking, meditating, reasoning
4. To seek after, aim at, strive after
5. To crave, demand something from someone

Spend time worshipping as you seek him for movement. Meditate in him, placing your mind, thoughts, and reasoning before him to be filled with his thoughts and plans. To seek in order to find means to be purposeful, intentional, and direct in what you are needing. Do not seek for just any movement. What you are seeking from God needs to be in alignment with the vision God is wanting you to release. This will make the vision of the dance clean and clear. Aim at, strive after, and put a demand on God to reveal his vision of movement.

Knock in the Strong's Concordance in this scripture means:

1. To rap
2. To knock at the door

Rap in Dictionary.com means:

1. To strike, especially with a quick, smart, or light blow
2. To utter sharply or vigorously
3. The sound produced by such a blow

You may have to war to breakthrough and receive movement.

- Speaking in fierce tongues while you are praying until there is a shift and breaking
- Decreeing and declaring out the purpose of the dance
- Praying over the people and region you will be ministering in - there may be demonic spirits connected to them that do not want them to receive what your ministry is releasing
- Decreeing out scripture that aligns with the purpose of the ministry

These are all strategies that can help you breakthrough to revelation and choreography.

Since you are aiming to create a visual of God's word through movement, the devil will send blockages because your movement will advance the kingdom.

When choreographing, you may experience blockages such as:

- You see nothing - white space or black space, emptiness. God revealed to us that this is called the spirit of void and darkness. Your eye gates, imagination, atmosphere and mind are all blank, dark, and empty. ***Genesis 1:2*** *The earth was without form and void, and darkness was over the face of the deep. And the Spirit of God was hovering over the face of the waters.*

- ❖ You will be executing movement one moment and the next moment it disappears from your mind and body. You cannot make progress because you keep forgetting the movement. This is called the zapping spirit. It strikes and jolts the movement from you. ***John 10:10*** *The thief comes only to steal and kill and destroy. I came that they may have life and have it abundantly.*
- ❖ It will feel like you are being blocked from receiving movement. This is a blocking spirit. A wall, barrier, or troop of demons that have locked themselves together in the spirit realm to hinder you from forward motion. ***Psalms 18:29*** *For by you I can run against a troop, and by my God I can leap over a wall.*
- ❖ You will feel confused, frustrated, disconnected from being able to understand and comprehend the movement. This is called the deaf and dumb spirit. It hinders your ability to see, hear, and fully grasp the movement. ***Mark 4:12*** *they may indeed see but not perceive, and may indeed hear but not understand, lest they should turn and be forgiven.*
- ❖ You do not receive anything because the song choice is not right.
- ❖ You might have good movements but it just does not feel right. However, you cannot put your finger on it.

Using these tools of prayer will help you break through these attacks purposed to hinder your progression in choreographing.

Posturing to receive from God through prayer draws you near to him. It allows you to connect with him and his spirit, which shifts you inside of his presence and inside of the spirit realm. You ascend to the throne room of God to receive what you are praying for (Hebrews 4:16). When you come into the throne room, you become seated in heavenly places with Jesus. You cease from the thoughts, familiarities, and limitations of your own mind. This realm grants you access to heavenly movement that is unlimited in creativity and power. Movement that is beyond this earth.

> **Ephesians 2:6 King James Version** *And hath raised us up together, and made us sit together in heavenly places in Christ Jesus:*
>
> **Colossians 3:1-2 King James Version** *If ye then be risen with Christ, seek those things which are above, where Christ sitteth on the right hand of God. Set your affection on things above, not on things on the earth.*

Above in the Strong's Concordance means:

1. Up, upwards, above, on high
2. Of the quarters of the heaven, northward
3. The word could refer to either place or time. Place- the Jerusalem which is above- in the heavens, time- the eternal Jerusalem which preceded the earthly one

You are seeking and receiving movement that is from above, on high, of the quarters of heaven.

Affection in the Strong's Concordance means:

1. Exercise the mind
2. To have understanding, be wise
3. To feel, to think
4. To have an opinion of one's self
5. To be of the same mind, agreed together, cherish the same views, be harmonious
6. To direct one's mind to a thing, to seek, to strive for

Receiving heavenly choreography from God is a state of mind. You must come into agreement and be harmonious with heaven. It is an exercise of the mind.

Earth in the Strong's Concordance means:

1. The ground, the earth as a standing place
2. The earth as a whole
3. The earth as opposed to the heavens
4. The inhabited earth, the abode of men and animals
5. A country, land enclosed within fixed boundaries, a tract of land, territory, region

Choreographing from an earthly stance limits you to the confines of man. You will only have access to what is fixed within the bounds of the land. The movements you have seen before, have done in the past, have received from other people, that are popular, will be the only movements you can see from an earthly perspective. When you set your state of mind on heaven becoming harmonious with it, you will bring the movement of heaven into the earth. Your choreography should fulfill the mandate of thy kingdom come, thy will be done on earth as it is in heaven. Choreography is not creating good moves, it is bringing the kingdom of heaven to earth through movement.

> ***Matthew 6:10 King James Version*** *Thy kingdom come. Thy will be done in earth, as it is in heaven.*

Each movement becomes a portal that connects heaven to earth, while releasing the royal authority and power of God to rule and reign in the lives of the people you are ministering to, and the regions and territories you are ministering in.

Come in the Strong's Concordance in this scripture means:

1. To come from one place to another
    - You translate heaven to earth
2. To appear, make one's appearance, come before the public
    - You cause heaven to appear before the people

3. To come into being, arise, come forth, show itself, find place or influence
    - You allow heaven to arise and find influence in the earth
4. Be established, become known
    - Knowledge of the kingdom becomes established

Will in the Strong's Concordance in this scripture means:

1. What one wishes or has determined shall be done
2. Of the purpose of God to bless mankind through Christ
3. Of what God wishes to be done by us- commands, precepts
4. Will, choice, inclination, desire, pleasure

We establish his commands, desires, and determinations as we embody his will in our movements.

Done in the Strong's Concordance in this scripture means:

1. Be brought to pass, be finished, be fulfilled
    - Doing a complete work of the will of God through your movement
2. Be published, be ordained to, be married to
    - Publishing, ordaining, and causing the will of God to marry earth
3. To appear in history
    - Should do an eternal and lasting work, leaving a mark in the people and regions
4. To be made finished- of miracles, to be performed wrought
    - The movement should produce the fruit of miracles and limitless possibilities of God

Once this realm of heaven is open in your mind:

- You will be able to receive movements that are unique, different, and have not been seen before.
- You will know that the movements are from God because of its nature and the power that flows as you execute it.
- You will receive movement that has revelation of God's will, purpose, and meaning infused into it.
- You will receive downloads from heaven to establish in the earth.

Publishing heaven in the people and regions you minister to is like Habakkuk 2:2 says, *"Write the vision, and make it plain upon tables"*. Plain in this scripture means that you dig, engrave, declare, make clear the vision of God through your choreography. And the tables are like the people and regions that you engrave it upon.

You can tell when movements are not from God when:

- ❖ It is dry, dull, stagnant and stale - lifeless
- ❖ There is no piercing or penetrating of the movement in the spirit
- ❖ There is no power or fortitude to it - even slower more intimate moves should be filled with power
- ❖ When it drags and lags behind - it feels like being in molasses
- ❖ When the music drowns it out rather than it dominating and governing the music
- ❖ When the movement is more of an improvising than actually fitting the song
- ❖ When it entails sensual or sexual innuendos - it does not have the character of God
- ❖ Has mixture and you can tell that there are worldly entanglements involved in it - lacks purity and holiness

- Has more of a "look at me" feel rather than a "look at God" and what he is doing through the movement
- It feels forced as if you had to come up with something more so than operating in the peace and flow of the Holy Spirit
- You keep going over it but keep forgetting certain parts - you get to a part and it either does not flow or just feels out of place
- You are hindered in choreographing further because that part is blocking true revelation from coming forth because it is not God's design

My Choreography Process

I begin my process by praying and asking God what the focus of the dance is. I ask him questions like:

- What are the people supposed to be receiving from the dance?
- What hindrances may block them from receiving what will be released through the dance?
- What is the condition of the people's hearts, minds, inner-man, and spirit who we will be ministering to?
- What is the atmosphere of their church, ministry, and region?
- What demonic spirits will we be combatting, if any?

Depending on what you are ministering for, all of these questions may not be applicable. These are just some examples of the questions I ask and pray about, especially when ministering abroad and outside of my home church. As I take the time to pray into these questions, God gives me clear descriptive answers to each of these. Now that I have the focus, I search for scriptures that align with the purpose of the ministry. This fills the movement with the power of the word of God. It builds and empowers my spirit as I study and meditate on them consistently, as I go throughout the preparation process, and all the way up to the ministry engagement. Since I know the direction God is taking the dance, I begin to look for songs that embody the vision. The song has to be able to help me bring forth the movement in fullness, and bring in a shift. This can take a little time, and that is okay because you want to find the song that includes all of the aspects God revealed to you. If you like the song but you know that it is not the "one," it is okay to keep listening and praying. God will give you the song.

Sometimes we will even minister to two songs and combine them one after the other. This helps to do a complete work and bring about a solidification. For example, one song may be breaking bondages off of people, while the song after it will be filling them back up with freedom and healing. God will lead you in being able to deliver the whole message and bring the full vision to pass. As I listen to the song, movements that go along with the vision fill my mind and my body. At times, as I am sitting down at work listening to the song to prepare for practice that week, I see movements in my mind. I jot down little notes to help me remember the moves for later when I can physically dance and activate the movements. Since I have already spent time in prayer, have clear descriptive vision, and filled myself with scripture, this part of the process can continue along with the flow. There will be times where you will have to pray through blockages as we discussed earlier in the chapter. It is always good to begin and end practice with prayer, whether it is personal practice or team practice. This helps to close you off from attacks and invites the Holy Spirit to reign and rain in your practice and move through your body.

When I get the chance to get up and dance, I piece together the movements that I saw in my mind. If they flow together when I minister them in my natural body, I keep them, and if they do not, I try out different movements that go along with that section until I find the ones that fit. When I do not have movements coming to my mind, I dance around freely with God and I put together the movements that stick. If I am having trouble finding a move that brings out what the song is saying and/or what God is doing at that section in the dance, I will pull out my phone and use Dictionary.com to look up the definitions of the words in the song, or what God is doing. I use the thesaurus as well to show me other words that describe it. This enhances my vision and aids me in being able to come up with unique and new movement. Manifold Grace Production Company ministered a dance where the song kept repeating "God is going to blow your mind." So I looked up the word blow and it was no longer just blow, it was a sudden hard stroke with the hand and fist, a weapon, a hurricane, a strong breeze! My spiritual imagination was flooded with movement after receiving that revelation and having my vision enhanced. I came up with multiple creative and unique movements and the dance was powerful.

As the process continues, I try out different moves and take risks with my body, trusting the Holy Spirit. Some things work and some things do not, and that is okay. Taking leaps to launch out into creativity will help you to grow in your choreography skill and enlarge your arsenal of movement. This way, you will not be bound to repeating the same movements over and over. You can set your spiritual imagination free, and give the Holy Spirit the opportunity to do in your body, things that you have never done, and would have never thought you could do. There are ladies on my team that have never had technical training before, but when they dance freely, there is no limitation to what they can do. I will have choreographed all types of turns, jumps, and leaps into the dance. When I show them, they give me the wide eyes, but when I teach them, and they begin to dance without fear, they execute the movements in excellence! Be okay to take risks, be creative, and let the Holy Spirit be limitless in you.

When I have developed a section of movement, I continue to build onto it until the dance is complete. In practice, as we minister the dance over and over we fine tooth comb through each movement and make sure that it is executed with power, precision, excellence, and genuine expression. The goal is not to merely do the movement, but to become the movement and embody the ability to plant it, reproduce it, and establish it.

Chapter 8
PURPOSE OF FASTING AS A DANCING MINISTER

By: Apostle Taquetta Baker

Fasting should be an important part of any believer's life, but for a dance minister it has added benefits that are essential to our ministry. As a dance minister, we embody the word of God. We carry the word of God in our mouths, in our bodies and in our spirit. We then release that word of God through movement.

For the dance minister, praise and worship is not just a Sunday fashion, it is our lifestyle. The very existence of who we are is a sign and representation of the presence of God. The scripture ***Joshua 1:3*** "*Every place that the sole of your foot shall tread upon, that have I given unto you, as I said unto Moses,*" is a literal mantle upon the dance minister. We are not just contending for God when we praise and worship, but every movement we make in our daily lives, contends for the glory of God. This is the reason warfare, struggle and persecution is constant for the dance minister. We are the glory of God moving about the earth - impregnating, revealing, creating, recreating, and establishing God's presence everywhere the soles of our feet tread.

Our posture regarding our bodies should be to be full of God. We should always desire to be free of demonic strongholds, curses, and cleansed of all worldliness, sin, and sickness. Repentance, deliverance, healing, and cleansing from anything that is not of God, should be a daily part of our lifestyle.

Fasting should also be a consistent part of our spiritual regimen because fasting kills the flesh - it subjects our flesh to our spirit so that as we live and minister, flesh does not glory in the presence of God (1Corinthians 1:29).

When flesh glory's it boasts, brags, rejoices, and exudes joy. It is not only revealing itself, but it is haughty in that it is bragging about being the ruler of us, while rejoicing that it has ahold of us - that it is stealing the glory of God through us. In some scriptures, the word glory means to bring renown fame which means to make famous. When flesh is glorying, it is being made famous through our lives and ministries rather than God being made famous through us.

We think because no one says anything or that because the boasting flesh is not blatant to people that it is undetected. However, when something is exalted it is released into the atmosphere. So even though people may not acknowledge or recognize that flesh is glorying, the atmosphere, demons, and God knows. They are not fooled or ignorant to what is being released - to what is boasting. The atmosphere takes on the aroma and formation of whatever is being released and carries it throughout the area. You can call it God's glory or contend you are giving God glory all you want, but if there are willing sins, demonic strongholds, and wickedness on the inside of you that is not being dealt with and being subjected to your spirit, that ungodliness is being distributed and published into the airways. That is what the atmosphere will radiate and that is what territorial spirits will grab ahold of to fortify their dominion over the people, the land, and the region.

This is the reason ***2Corinthians 10:4-5*** says, *"For the weapons of our warfare are not carnal, but mighty through God to the pulling down of strong holds; Casting down imaginations, and every high thing that exalteth itself against the knowledge of*

God, and bringing into captivity every thought to the obedience of Christ."

When you think your flesh cannot be seen you are operating in vain imagination. Your body is presenting a case and argument against strongholds that it cannot win because the weapon of God's truth is not in you.

In the Old Testament, the praise and worship ministry was all about being consecrated and set a part for the glory of God. They had a conscious understanding that they lived in, ministered unto, served, and embodied the presence of God. They possessed a reverence for God because they knew his presence could be taken away, as it was a privilege to have God dwell in and among them.

> ***Psalms 51:10*** *Create in me a clean heart, O God; and renew a right spirit within me.*

Fasting demonstrates a reverenced fear and intense desire to be consecrated unto the Lord. It displays a desire to please the Lord, offer the best of you unto him, and a willingness to position yourself to be used by him. You are willingly offering yourself as a sacrifice - killing yourself - so that God can live and reign in you. Fasting is never going to be easy, because when we sacrifice something, we are surrendering that which is desirable or treasured.

In the Old Testament, even though an animal was going to be killed, you could not offer up a lame or defected animal as sacrifice unto the Lord. God wanted the best animal sacrificed unto him. Yet when we fast, we at times want to offer a blemished, lame or blind sacrifice. Not our best sacrifice, but that which we are willing to part ways with and only for that time of consecration. This is interesting because when something is killed, you cannot get it back, yet we rarely fast to truly rid ourselves of something. We often return to that thing and resurrect it after our time of consecration has ended. We did not sacrifice it. We just sustained from it for a period of time.

> ***Deuteronomy 15:21*** *And if there be any blemish therein, as if it be lame, or blind, or have any ill blemish, thou shalt not sacrifice it unto the LORD thy God.*

> ***Leviticus 1:9*** *If his offering be a burnt sacrifice of the herd, let him offer a male without blemish: he shall offer it of his own voluntary will at the door of the tabernacle of the congregation before the LORD.*

This is probably some of the reason our deliverance and healing is not sustained. Our fasting sacrifice is defected. It is the bare minimum rather than our best offering unto God - an offering we are willing to kill to show honor unto God.

When we give the bare minimum or leftovers, we are giving God something we are willing to sacrifice, rather than something that will cost us something to sacrifice. We are also not trusting God to replenish and restore. In the Old Testament, when they offered up their best animal, they had to trust that God would give them greater than what they sacrificed, otherwise they would not have food or even flock that provided provision.

> ***Malachi I:13-14 The Message Bible*** *And when you say, 'I'm bored – this doesn't do anything for me.' You act so superior, sticking your noses in the air – act superior to me, God-of-the-Angel-Armies! And when you do offer something to me, it's a hand-me-down, or broken, or useless. Do you think I'm going to accept it? This is God speaking to you! "A curse on the person who makes a big show of doing something great for me – an*

expensive sacrifice, say – and then at the last minute brings in something puny and worthless! I'm a great king, God-of-the-Angel-Armies, honored far and wide, and I'll not put up with it!

God is appalled by defected sacrifices. He does not receive them neither does he receive flesh glorying in his presence. No matter how much we are seeking to impress him and others, God is not impressed. We must make sure we are giving him our best sacrifice so it can be received, and so that our ministry of dance can ascribe unto him the honor and glory due his name.

> ***Psalms 29:1-2*** *The Message Bible Bravo, God, bravo! Gods and all angels shout, "Encore!" In awe before the glory, in awe before God's visible power. Stand at attention! Dress your best to honor him!*
>
> ***The Amplified Bible*** *ASCRIBE TO the Lord, O sons of the mighty, ascribe to the Lord glory and strength. Give to the Lord the glory due to His name; worship the Lord in the beauty of holiness or in holy array.*

- ✓ As a dancer, is fasting a part of your lifestyle?
- ✓ Are you giving God your best sacrifice when you fast?
- ✓ What do you really need to kill to totally submit in reverence to God during your fasts and in your life as a whole?
- ✓ Do you trust God to give you greater than what you are sacrificing when you fast?

Decreeing great fruit in your dance ministry and life as you SHIFT to a lifestyle of consistent fasting, consecration, and sacrificing of self unto the Lord! SHIFT!

Chapter 9
Heavenly Garments
By: Minister Nina Cook

Exodus 28:3 King James Version *And thou shalt speak unto all that are wise hearted, whom I have filled with the spirit of wisdom, that they may make Aaron's garments to consecrate him, that he may minister unto me in the priest's office.*

New Living Translation
Instruct all the skilled craftsmen whom I have filled with the spirit of wisdom. Have them make garments for Aaron that will distinguish him as a priest set apart for my service.

Amplified Bible
Tell all who are expert, whom I have endowed with skill and good judgment, that they shall make Aaron's garments to sanctify him for My priesthood.

Our selection of garments should be guided by wisdom and inspiration from the Lord. The garments that Aaron and his sons wore distinguished them for the service of priesthood. The skilled craftsmen were experts in their trade, and were endowed by God with good judgment and wisdom to create the priestly garments by God's design. In this same manner, we should be seeking God's wisdom for what we should be clothed with that is distinct to our ministry and service unto Him.

Your garments should set you a part!

They should consecrate and dedicate you to a service!

Consecrate from Dictionary.com means:

1. To make or declare sacred; set apart or dedicate to the service of a deity: *to consecrate a new church building.*
2. To make (something) an object of honor or veneration; hallow:
3. To devote or dedicate to some purpose:
4. To admit or ordain to a sacred office, especially to the episcopate.

Your garments declare you as sacred, esteem your ministry, dedicate you to God, and shift you into divine office. They admit and ordain you to whatever position God has called you to. When we are putting on our garments, are we thinking that we are literally stepping into rank and are being ordained for a specific service in an office? Each time you go forth in dance and allow God to lead you in your garment choice, you are stepping into the endowment of power for that individual assignment. DEEP!

People should be able to distinguish you from others, recognize who you are and what you are doing by your garments. By Aaron's garments, they knew he was a priest, therefore, people's actions toward him aligned with who they knew he was. They regarded him as holy, pure, sacred, sanctified and to be revered. People should be able to see who you are in God by your garments and bring honor and respect upon your ministry. People will begin to view you differently, interact with you differently, and receive of you differently as they recognize and acknowledge your mantle. The mantle will speak for you and identify you. It is the embodiment of who you are. It is your covering and protects, conceals, coats, and fortifies you in what you need to go forth. It is a literal part of YOU.

Your garments should:

- ❖ Align with and match what your service is. Aaron and his sons were called to the service and office of priest so their garments were priestly.
- ❖ Be inspired by the Lord.
- ❖ Be guided by Gods wisdom and instruction, the skilled craftsmen were instructed, endowed, filled and inspired.
- ❖ Be crafted well and by someone who is skilled in this area. Anyone should not just be making your garments- this also goes to show that you should take care of your garments. If they are old or raggedy they are no longer fit for use because good craftsmanship and excellency should always be evident.

> **Exodus 28:1** *And take thou unto thee Aaron thy brother, and his sons with him, from among the children of Israel, that he may minister unto me in the priest's office, even Aaron, Nadab and Abihu, Eleazar and Ithamar, Aaron's sons.*

The revelation of who you are and what your service is should come before you are clothed or garmented. Before they put on the garments, they were first told they were coming into the office of priest. They had a revelation of who they were and what they were stepping into. You must know who you are first and what you are called to do, in order to know what you should be clothed in. The mantle should match the call on your life.

> **Exodus 28:4** *And these are the garments which they shall make; a breastplate, and an ephod, and a robe, and a broidered coat, a mitre, and a girdle:and they shall make holy garments for Aaron thy brother, and his sons, that he may minister unto me in the priest's office.*

Amplified Bible
They shall make these garments: a breastplate, an ephod [a distinctive vestment to which the breastplate was to be attached], a robe, long and sleeved tunic of checkerwork, a turban, and a sash or band. They shall make sacred garments for Aaron your brother and his sons to minister to me in the priest's office.

Each piece of clothing they were instructed to wear displayed priestly royalty, dignity, and authority. They matched the calling and service on their lives.

When you have an assignment or ministry from the Lord, there are certain things you need to be clothed and armored with to help you and cover you, as you fulfill the assignment.

Jesus assignment:

1 John 3:8 *He that committeth sin is of the devil; for the devil sinneth from the beginning. For this purpose the Son of God was manifested, that he might destroy the works of the devil.*

Isaiah 59:17-18 *For he put on righteousness as a breastplate, and an helmet of salvation upon his head; and he put on the garments of vengeance for clothing, and was clad with zeal as a cloke. According to their deeds, accordingly he will repay, fury to his adversaries, recompence to his enemies; to the islands he will repay recompence.*

New Living Translation
He put on righteousness as his body armor and placed the helmet of salvation on his head. He clothed himself with a robe of vengeance and wrapped himself in a cloak of divine passion. He will repay his enemies for their evil

deeds. His fury will fall on his foes. He will pay them back even to the ends of the earth.

Jesus' assignment was to destroy the works of the devil. He clothed himself in vengeance and wrapped himself in divine passion to be destructive and avenging against the enemy. He needed to be mantled with these qualities to fulfill God's will for His life.

When you minister, you must ask and seek God for what you need to be armored with to fulfill his will for your ministry. Doing this causes his covering to increase because you are being concealed and wrapped in attributes of Him. You are literally putting on God. Ephesians 6:11-17 empowers us with this revelation. Jesus himself embodies each of these components of the whole armor of God.

> ***Ephesians 6:11-17*** *Put on the whole armour of God, that ye may be able to stand against the wiles of the devil. For we wrestle not against flesh and blood, but against principalities, against powers, against the rulers of the darkness of this world, against spiritual wickedness in high places. Wherefore take unto you the whole armour of God, that ye may be able to withstand in the evil day, and having done all, to stand. Stand therefore, having your loins girt about with truth, and having on the breastplate of righteousness; And your feet shod with the preparation of the gospel of peace; Above all, taking the shield of faith, wherewith ye shall be able to quench all the fiery darts of the wicked. And take the helmet of salvation, and the sword of the Spirit, which is the word of God;*

1. "Stand therefore having your loins girt about with truth"
   Jesus is the truth.

- ***John 14:6*** *Jesus saith unto him, I am the way, the truth, and the life:no man cometh unto the Father, but by me.*

2. "And having on the breastplate of righteousness" ***Jesus is righteousness.***

- ***1 Corinthians 1:30*** *And because of him you are in Christ Jesus, who became to us wisdom from God, righteousness and sanctification and redemption,*
- ***2 Corinthians 5:21*** *For our sake he made him to be sin who knew no sin, so that in him we might become the righteousness of God.*

3. "And your feet shod with the preparation of the gospel of peace" ***Jesus is the gospel of peace.***

- ***Mark 1:1-3*** *The beginning of the gospel of Jesus Christ, the Son of God. As it is written in Isaiah the prophet, "Behold, I send my messenger before your face, who will prepare your way, the voice of one crying in the wilderness: 'Prepare the way of the Lord, make his paths straight,'"*

4. "Above all, taking the shield of faith, wherewith ye shall be able to quench all the fiery darts of the wicked." ***Jesus is the source of our faith.***

- ***Hebrews 12:2*** *Looking unto Jesus the author and finisher of our faith; who for the joy that was set before him endured the cross, despising the shame, and is set down at the right hand of the throne of God.*

5. "And take the helmet of salvation" ***Jesus is our Salvation.***

- ***Psalms 27:1*** *The Lord is my light and my salvation; whom shall I fear? the Lord is the strength of my life; of whom shall I be afraid?*

6. "And the sword of the Spirit, which is the word of God:
   Jesus is the word.

John 1:1 *In the beginning was the Word, and the Word was with God, and the Word was God.*

We see from these scriptures that when you are putting on your armor, you are being covered in Jesus.

We must have true meaning and purpose for our garments because it is our armor. When your focus for choosing garments is solely based on what looks good, what is popular, what flatters your team members and etc., you are not able to receive direction from the Lord on what your choice should be (you should look nice and presentable in your garments, however, looking good should not be your sole focus). You also put yourself and team at risk because you believe you are covered when you are not. Without true meaning and purpose, you are merely wearing a costume causing you to minister from a form of godliness and even idolatry, as the focus is not about God or your service to Him, but you. The difference between wearing purposeful heavenly garments and costumes is crucial because it separates us from secular arts and the world. It distinguishes you as a true minister whose dance is about releasing the will of God.

- ✓ The clothing should not be about you. It is not about having a higher status than others or what type of position or prominence you can gain by wearing garments. It is not even about the garment itself, but the purpose, meaning, covering and mantle of it all.

James 2:2-3 *For if there come unto your assembly a man with a gold ring, in goodly apparel, and there come in also a poor man in vile raiment; And ye have respect to him that weareth the gay clothing, and say unto him, Sit thou here in a good place; and say to the poor, Stand thou there, or sit here under my footstool:*

- ✓ Wearing garments that look nice and like they are right does not necessarily mean that they are God.

Matthew 7:15 *Beware of false prophets, which come to you in sheep's clothing, but inwardly they are ravening wolves.*

Mark 12:38-40 *And he said unto them in his doctrine, Beware of the scribes, which love to go in long clothing, and love salutations in the marketplaces, And the chief seats in the synagogues, and the uppermost rooms at feasts: Which devour widows 'houses, and for a pretence make long prayers:these shall receive greater damnation.*

- ✓ You should be clothed in what will bring forth effective fruit of your ministry. If God sends you to minister a refreshing rain and tells you to wear a garment that looks like the rain of heaven, this fruit will follow as you minister. He gave you that instruction because He knew it would cover you and help you be all the more effective in releasing the rain.

Luke 24:46-49 English Standard Version *and said to them, "Thus it is written, that the Christ should suffer and on the third day rise from the dead, and that repentance and forgiveness of sins should be proclaimed* *in his name to all nations, beginning from Jerusalem. You are witnesses of these things. And behold, I am sending the promise of my Father upon you. But stay in the city until you are clothed with power from on high."*

In this scripture, the disciples learned they were called to be witnesses of the gospel. They are instructed to wait to be clothed in power before they went forth in their assignment. They needed the fruit of power to be effective in their ministry to be witnesses of the gospel.

Endued

- In the sense of sinking into a garment
- To invest with clothing
- Array, clothe, have put on
- To sink into (clothing), put on, clothe one's self

Power

- Force
- Miraculous power
- Ability, abundance, meaning
- Might, worker of miracles
- Power, strength, violence
- Inherent power, power residing in a thing by virtue of its nature, or which a person or thing exerts and puts forth
- Power for performing miracles
- Moral power and excellence of soul
- The power and influence which belongs to riches and wealth
- Power and resources

They were endued with limitless and miraculous power because it matched the calling Jesus released to them, and it was sufficient covering for the depth of ministry they were shifting into. They could not go forth preaching and proclaiming the gospel without the garmenting of the Holy Spirit and power.

Questions to reflect on:

1. Do my garments match the depth of the assignment God has called me too?

2. Do my garments have the fruit of God? And do they have the specific fruits to which I need to be effective for that particular ministry assignment?

Chapter 10
MINISTERING FROM HEAVENLY PLACES DURING PRAISE & WORSHIP

By: Apostle Taquetta Baker

Topics Explored In This Chapter:

- ✓ Ministering As One Army
- ✓ Dancing With Intentionality
- ✓ Dancing In The Spirit
- ✓ Governing The Atmosphere

This chapter will explore how to minister beyond the realm of a general praise and worship dancer, as many are called to that sphere of influence. This chapter, however, will explore how to operate as an army during praise and worship to see deliverance, healing, and breakthrough manifest in people, atmospheres, regions, and the ministry or event you are ministering for.

As a dance ministry, we enter praise and worship as one army. When you minister as an army, you are seeking to overthrow the enemy, while opening and governing the heavenlies so the presence of the Lord can reign and work in your midst. Therefore, moves are ministered in sets of 4, 8, 12 and at times are repetitious, as they are easy to follow and allows us to attack the enemy and take up territory as one army. The enemy hates unity and agreement as he cannot penetrate it. Even if one or two people feel led to do something unique apart from the team, it is important to communicate that so we can cover you. As when ministering during praise and worship, you are on a battle ground fighting for the people, the atmosphere, the community and the region. Every move you make and sound you make is heard by the enemy and they will counterattack with war in effort to contend for their desire to remain in the lives of the people, govern the heavenlies, while strong holding the community and region. Every church service, conference, event, etc., should be designed to establish the kingdom of God in people and the earth. The devil knows this even if we do not know this - even if we do not recognize we are contending for the kingdom of God, we are and the battle is waging whether we acknowledge it, engage it as such, or want to fight.

> ***Matthew 11:12*** *Baptist until now the kingdom of heaven suffereth violence, and the violent take it by force.*

During praise and worship, our initial movement should be done through ***Ephesians 2:6*** "*And hath raised us up together, and made us sit together in heavenly places in Christ Jesus.*" We seek to dance from the heavenly realms and not from the earth realm. Therefore, our initial focus is not the music or song played, but getting into the spirit where we can govern the atmosphere and flowing in movement is easy. So even if the singers start with a praise song, and we begin to minister, if we are not able to enter into the spirit realm after a couple of minutes, then we may have to minister warfare or intercessory movements to SHIFT us in the heavenlies.

Initial movements must also have a focus of moving darkness and demonic forces out the way, so we can open the heavens for God's glory to reign.

> ***Jeremiah 1:10*** *See, I have this day set thee over the nations and over the kingdoms, to root out, and to pull down, and to destroy, and to throw down, to build, and to plant.*

This is so important because ***Ephesians 6:12*** lets us know that "*We wrestle not against flesh and blood, but against* *principalities, against powers, against the rulers of the darkness of this world, against spiritual wickedness in high places."-*

When the dancing R&B singer Beyonce comes on stage, her initial focus is to own the stage and the people, and to assert authority over the atmosphere. Her song and movements, even how she walks on stage, demonstrates and asserts her purpose. It does not matter if you like the song, the words, or the movement, you will be drawn into her because she seeks to claim dominion over the atmosphere and the people. Beyonce knows her dominion, her authority, and she knows her power.

As dance ministers and saints of Jesus, we already have dominion and power over people, atmospheres, regions and devils.

> ***Genesis 1:26*** *And God said, Let us make man in our image, after our likeness: and let them have dominion over the fish of the sea, and over the fowl of the air, and over the cattle, and over all the earth, and over every creeping thing that creepeth upon the earth.*

> ***Genesis 9:2*** *And the fear of you and the dread of you shall be upon every beast of the earth, and upon every fowl of the air, upon all that moveth upon the earth, and upon all the fishes of the sea; into your hand are they delivered.*

> ***Psalm 8:6*** *Thou madest him to have dominion over the works of thy hands; thou hast put all things under his feet.*

> ***Hebrews 2:8*** *Thou hast put all things in subjection under his feet. For in that he put all in subjection under him, he left nothing that is not put under him. But now we see not yet all things put under him.*

James 3:7 *For every kind of beasts, and of birds, and of serpents, and of things in the sea, is tamed, and hath been tamed of mankind.*

Luke 10:19 *Behold, I give unto you power to tread on serpents and scorpions, and over all the power of the enemy: and nothing shall by any means hurt you.*

Psalms 2:8 *Ask of me, and I shall give thee the heathen for thine inheritance, and the uttermost parts of the earth for thy possession.*

Psalms 18:39-44 *For thou hast girded me with strength unto the battle: thou hast subdued under me those that rose up against me. Thou hast also given me the necks of mine enemies; that I might destroy them that hate me. They cried, but there was none to save them: even unto the Lord, but he answered them not.*

Psalms 144:2 *My goodness, and my fortress; my high tower, and my deliverer; my shield, and he in whom I trust; who subdueth my people under me.*

A lot of times we are striving to acquire dominion, authority and power by whether the people and atmosphere receives us. However, we must know our dominion and power before we come before the people. Our position cannot change regardless to how the people respond or the warfare that occurs in the spirit realm.

When you are ministering from a place of dominion and power you cannot be:

- Unintentional where you are just going through the motions, ministering through laziness or sluggardness
- Fearful
- Insecure

- Have low or no self and God confidence

You must be:

- Intentional
- Precise and clear in your movement
- Trusting of your team and flowing from your spirit man where you can follow with ease, strength and purpose
- Bold and authoritative
- Confident
- Secure that you were chosen and equipped for the assignment

Please understand that the devil is always intentional. ***1Peter 5:8*** says, *"Be sober, be vigilant; because your adversary the devil, as a roaring lion, walketh about, seeking whom he may devour."*

Devour means to *"consume destructively, recklessly or wantonly (deliberately) – to totally engulf."* The devil is on the prow to overthrow, kill, steal, destroy and totally devour, such that there is not any inkling that you ever existed and what you did for God was a part of the earth. This is the mindset we must take for the kingdom of God. We must be so driven to take this world by force where everything we do has such a divine impact, that it is like the devil never existed and was ever a factor in this world.

Let us talk about intentionality for a moment, as it is key to operating in dominion and power.

Dictionary.com defines *intentional* as:

1. done with intention or on purpose; intended
2. of or relating to intention or purpose pertaining to the capacity of the mind to refer to an existent or nonexistent object.

3. pointing beyond itself, as consciousness or a sign.

Being intentional does not mean doing a dance harder or sharper. Though that is important, intentional means dancing on purpose with purpose.

- What is the purpose of praise and worship for that assignment and for that day?
- What does God want to do in the land, region, atmosphere, people in that service, community, region and even nation as the assignment can be narrow and even that broad at times.
- What are your weapons for the day?
    - Movements
    - Revelation and vision of God's plan for that service or event
    - Flags
    - Tambourines and praise hoops
    - Mishkans, billows, glory shawls
    - Staffs, rods, and swords
    - Shofars
    - Crowns
    - Banners

  These weapons are always necessary and vital to you being an effective army. A soldier is not looking around for his gun when he is in the middle of a war. Having them available and ready for use is key to effective warfare. Knowing which weapons are needed at the beginning of the battle or having your arsenal ready even if you are unsure of what you will need, is key to overthrowing the enemy and opening or asserting authority over the heavenlies quickly.

- What are your weapons as far as movement in overtaking the territory quickly and asserting your God given authority over the people, land, atmosphere, and region?

- Do you go in like a stealth bomber? A stealth bomber goes in subtle and undetected then -blasts the enemy, so your movements will be subtle and unassuming. As the Holy Spirit leads, you shift and begin to blast the enemy with warfare movements. ***Psalms 18:28-29*** *For thou wilt light my candle: the Lord my God will enlighten my darkness. For by thee I have run through a troop; and by my God have I leaped over a wall.*

- Do you send in some snipers or does everyone enter in as snipers and your movement annihilate the enemy in sniper fashion? Snipers hide or move about strategically where you blend in the environment. Your focus and intent is to discern your target, then take them out quickly. ***Joshua 23:10*** *One man of you shall chase a thousand: for the Lord your God, he it is that fighteth for you, as he hath promised you. Chase (radap)* in this scripture means, *"to pursue, hunt, attend closely to, persecute, put to flight."* Therefore, you may appear to be flowing with the praise and worship team where you are ministering movements related to the song, yet your focus is on demolishing the target. Some targets could be sniping out religion, tradition, heaviness, witchcraft, sluggardness, python, leviathan, mixture, confusion, death, etc.

- Do you minister through the power of the Lord and minister movements that chase down your enemy? ***Leviticus 26:8*** *And five of you shall chase an hundred, and an hundred of you shall put ten thousand to flight: and your enemies shall fall before you by the sword.* This is different than a sniper as you are operating through the power, force and promise of God. You are also chasing out whatever is in your way -whatever is clogging up the land, atmosphere and heavenlies - whatever is hindering the presence of God from freely flowing.

- Do you dance and move from a place of ambushing the enemy? When you ambush, there has to be a plan from the Lord of how to take your enemy out. Often these are given to someone in the ministry days ahead of time or before a service, but can also be given during praise and worship. God may tell you all to dance from the back rather than starting in the front. He may have you station flaggers at the four corners of the room. He may have some dancers ministering the isles, while some are ministering in the front. You first must know that as dance ministers you can ambush the enemy, then you must be open to the unique plans of the Lord. He will use the foolish to confound the wise so what he will have you to do will be out of the box and norm of how you would traditionally enter praise and worship. However, his plan is for the purposes of ambushing your enemy so you can establish his kingdom in your midst. ***Jeremiah 51:12*** *Lift up a signal against the walls of Babylon; Post a strong guard, Station sentries, Place men in ambush! For the LORD has both purposed and performed What He spoke concerning the inhabitants of Babylon.*

Joshua 8:3-25 *So Joshua rose with all the people of war to go up to Ai; and Joshua chose 30,000 men, valiant warriors, and sent them out at night. He commanded them, saying, "See, you are going to ambush the city from behind it. Do not go very far from the city, but all of you be ready. "Then I and all the people who are with me will approach the city. And when they come out to meet us as at the first, we will flee before them).*

- Do you decree and declare through movement? These are commanding and establishing movements. Examples would be pointing, directing demons out, using your hands and feet as daggers or swords to direct or establish the authority of God in your midst such that it annihilates the enemy, while asserting your divine authority in the name and power of the Lord through movement ***(Job 22:28*** *You shall decree a thing and it is established).*

- Do you stand on and minister through the word of God? You can have a scripture that everyone is told before praise and worship begins or even during service, so they will know what the focus is while dancing; you can use the word to divide what is God and what is not of God and minister movements in this fashion. You can stand on who you are in God as a glory carrying warrior, or on the words of encouragement, knowledge, prophesy, etc., that is being released during praise and worship. ***Psalms 119:105*** *Thy word is a lamp unto my feet, and a light unto my path.*

  Hebrews 4:12-13 *For the word of God is quick [living], and powerful [active], and sharper than any twoedged sword, piercing even to the dividing asunder of soul and spirit, and of the joints and marrow, and is a discerner and judge of the thoughts and intents of the heart.*

- Do you use the power and execution of praise to judge and wreak vengeance on the enemy? Soldiers are quiet at times but they also shout, yell, sound alarms, etc. You can also sound alarms and execute judgement through movements of high praise and abandoned praise and worship. High praises serve as double edge swords against the enemy. ***Psalms 149*** *Let the high praises of God be in their throats and a two-edged sword in* *their hands, To wreak vengeance upon the nations and chastisement upon the peoples, To bind their kings with chains, and their nobles with fetters of iron, To execute upon them the judgment written. He [the Lord] is the honor of all His saints. Praise the Lord! (Hallelujah!)*

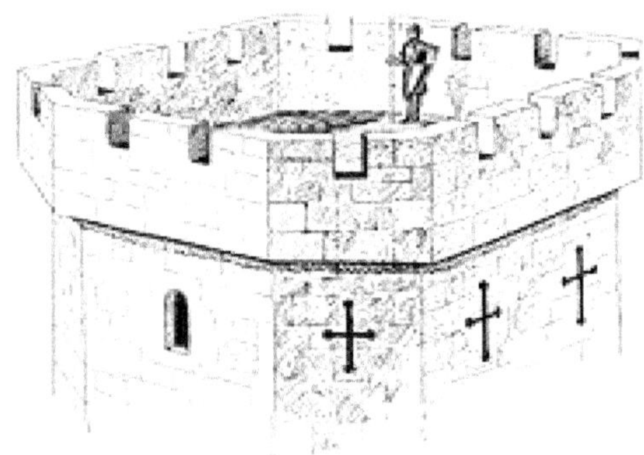

- Do you dance inside the refuge, strength and fortress of the glory, and allow your praise and worship to annihilate the enemy? ***Psalms 91:7-8*** *thousand may fall at your side, and ten thousand at your right hand, but it shall not come near you. Only a spectator shall you be [yourself inaccessible in the secret place of the Most High] as you witness the reward of the wicked.* **Psalms 84:11** *God is a sun and shield: the LORD will give grace and glory: no good thing will he withhold from them that walk uprightly.* If you study the word sun from ***Psalms 84:11*** you will find that one of its definitions is *notched battlement*. A *notch battlement* is *"a castle, fort, or other military fortification, a battlement is the top part of the wall that looks like teeth."* It is where soldiers are protected during "battle." This is actually a place we should live as glory carriers, but for the sake of this lesson, since we are spirit beings and living in heavenly places, we can enter inside the notch battlement by faith and dance and war from this fortification.

- Do you recognize that the enemy has already overtaken and now you have to enter praise and worship by smiting, terrorizing, traumatizing, and ripping the enemy to shreds? ***Deuteronomy 28:7*** *The LORD shall cause thine enemies that rise up against thee to be smitten before thy face: they shall come out against thee one way, and flee before thee seven ways.*

Intentional is a mindset and understanding of how to demonstrate and implement the word of God and the warfare tactics of God into movement. Dance ministers who want to flow beyond that of a praiser or worshipper, must understand that we are warriors that carry the presence of God, and that praise and worship must be approached through the posture of taking the kingdom by force.

Jeremiah 51:20 *Thou are my battle axe and weapons of war: for with you will I break in pieces the nations, and with you will I destroy kingdoms.*

Isaiah 41:15-16 *Behold, I will make thee a new sharp threshing instrument having teeth: thou shalt thresh the mountains, and beat them small, and shalt make the hills as chaff. Thou shalt fan them, and the wind shall carry them away, and the whirlwind shall scatter them: and thou shalt rejoice in the Lord, and shalt glory in the Holy One of Israel.*

Psalms 7:11-13 *God judgeth the righteous, and God is angry with the wicked every day. If he turn not, he will whet his sword; he hath bent his bow, and made it ready. He hath also prepared for him the instruments of death; he ordaineth his arrows against the persecutors.*

Jeremiah 50:25 *The Lord has opened up his armoury, and hath brought forth the weapons of his indignation (fury and* *wrath): for this is the work of the Lord GOD of hosts in the land of the Chaldeans.*

Job 38:21-23 *Hast thou entered into the treasures of the snow? or hast thou seen the treasures of the hail, Which I have reserved against the time of trouble, against the day of battle and war?*

The Message Bible *Have you ever traveled to where snow is made, seen the vault where hail is stockpiled, The arsenals of hail and snow that I keep in readiness for times of trouble and battle and war?*

In this scripture, treasures mean store house of armor, snow halts, discomfits and freezes things and hail releases judgment and destruction. God is saying have you entered the store houses where I prepare and make my weapons and do you even realize that I have been preparing you in my store houses of armor for such a time as this. The dance ministers being released in this season, are weapons from heaven's store house of armor. He has prepared instruments of death – warring glory carriers for such a time as this.

> **Psalms 144:1** *Blessed be the LORD my strength, which teacheth my hands to war, and my fingers to fight.*
>
> **Psalms 18:34** *He teacheth my hands to war, so that a bow of steel is broken by mine arms.*

Intentional dance is not what you feel, but is beyond feelings, emotions or desires. Being intentional is

- Seeing beyond
- Being conscious to sense beyond
- Seeing God's spiritual signs as these are signs beyond what the people show you, what is in the natural atmosphere, the song being ministered

- Moving beyond your natural ability as a dance minister where God dictates the movements

Intentionality is drawing from the intent of the Holy Spirit, while operating in your dominion and power as a frontline intercessor through dance for God's glory.

Being intentional is also knowing you are a spiritual sign and being aligned with God so that you are a sign of what he desires the people, land, region, atmosphere to receive for that particular setting. You only can achieve this level of ministry from the spirit realm as the word says:

> ***2Corinthians 3:17*** *Now the Lord is that Spirit: and where the Spirit of the Lord is, there is liberty.*
>
> ***John 4:24*** *God is a spirit and they that worship him must worship him in spirit and in truth.*

We know that liberty and truth breeds freedom, clarity, direction of the Lord and his will, and the ability to see and discern things from his perspective.

Discernment is *kritikos* in the Greek and means, "*decisive ("critical"), i.e. discriminative. discerner, relating to judging, fit for judging, skilled.*"

It means judicial estimation, discern, disputation. It comes from a word meaning to separate thoroughly, withdraw, oppose, discriminate, decide, hesitate, contend, make to differ, doubt, judge, be partial, stagger, waver. When one discerns they are disputing, opposing, hesitating, contending, differing, doubting, staggering, and wavering against that which appears to be right but is not right, appears to be God but is not of God, or is an enemy of God. Discernment is an internal war as one grapples to line up what they perceive, with Who God is, and what is being offered as truth or liberty.

This brings us back to ***Jeremiah 1:10*** where God was establishing the prophet over the nations to overthrow kingdoms, to root out, and to pull down, and to destroy, and to throw down, to build, and to plant.

If you read this book of the bible, you will find that Jeremiah needed, intentionality, confidence, boldness and keen discernment to complete this assignment. He had to know his right as a prophet and his dominion, authority and power as God's chosen vessel.

> ***Hebrews 5:13-14*** *For every one that useth milk is unskilful in the word of righteousness: for he is a babe. But strong meat belongeth to them that are of full age, even those who by reason of use have their senses exercised to discern both good and evil.*

Exercised in the Greek is *gymnazō* and means, *"To practice naked (in the games), to be trained, (in a palaestra or school of athletics), to exercise vigorously, in any way, either the body or the mind."*

> ***The Amplified Bible*** *But solid food is for full-grown men, for those whose senses and mental faculties are trained by practice to discriminate and distinguish between what is morally good and noble and what is evil and contrary either to divine or human law.*

> ***Hebrews 4:12-13*** *For the word of God is quick [living], and powerful [active], and sharper than any twoedged sword, piercing even to the dividing asunder of soul and spirit, and of the joints and marrow, and is a discerner and judge of the thoughts and intents of the heart.*

Before you start ministering in dance and while you are dancing, you should be discerning God for his intent so that you can release his heart, motive and will into the people, atmosphere and region. That means your assignment does not start when you get to the service, but in your private prayer, study, and training time with the Lord. As you dance, you already know your dominion, authority, and power and as you focus on pulling down strongholds and opening the heavens, everything becomes subjected to you. You know you have established yourself in heavenly places because movements become easy and you are able to praise and worship from a supernatural place of joy, freedom and truth.

- Joy in basking inside the presence of the Lord
- Freedom from the contending of strongholds, demons, witchcraft, confusion, heaviness, oppression and depression
- Truth that God's spirit is the only spirit that is reigning and ruling

Sometimes we will accomplish this place then relax. Especially when deliverance, healing, breakthrough, and transformation begins to manifest in the people, ground, atmosphere and region. This is to be expected as ***Psalms 16:11*** lets us know that *"in his presence is fullness of joy and at his right hand are pleasures for every more."* However, seated in heavenly places means to be established, to govern, and is an actual office. Therefore, it is a place of conquering. To maintain our office, we have to work, maintain and sustain in our position. It is not a time to become lazy and sluggard, lest the enemy overtake us and regain the territory we worked so hard to achieve. So even though we can now be more in tune with what the praise and worship team is ministering, dance through their leading, and even partake of what God is doing in our midst, we still need to be cognizant and discerning that we are keeping the spiritual gates secure of anything that would try to retaliate or sneak in. An army may celebrate their victory, but their weapon is always in their hand.

> **Exodus 15:20-21** *And Miriam the prophetess, the sister of Aaron, took a timbrel in her hand; and all the women went out after her with timbrels and with dances. And Miriam answered them, Sing ye to the Lord, for he hath triumphed gloriously; the horse and his rider hath he thrown into the sea.*

Chapter 11

NUGGETS FOR DANCING AS AN ARMY DURING PRAISE AND WORSHIP

By: Apostle Taquetta Baker & Minister Nina Cook

Make sure you are dancing in a window. Unless the formation requires it, do not stand (hide) directly behind someone. If there are more than two ministers dancing at one time, do not dance in a straight line.

Use the isles and be open to move throughout the entire room as the spirit leads.

Use your space and dance with your entire body, not just with your hands.

Whoever is leading should be ministering in the front middle area where every dance team member can see them.

Always seek to maintain eye contact with one another. Both during transitions so that we can stay in unity with our movements and when you leave to take a break as well. This way if there are two or more of you that have left you can find a way to enter back into the dance space together by doing the same movement to rejoin the group.

Be attentive and aware of the whereabouts of each member. This helps us to be able to receive instruction at the same time, know when we are going on and off to minister, and be in unity with one another. This will alleviate confusion and discord, and will keep us operating as one and in excellence.

Minister movements in sets of 4, 8, 12 and so forth. This is so the dance ministers can follow you sufficiently. Be okay with repetitious movements. Be cognizant that your team is and can clearly discern and follow your movements, while receiving revelation of what God is doing through the movements. Generally, when movements are difficult to follow, the team does not have sufficient revelation, the movements are not God led, or the enemy is infiltrating the unity of the team. Be more concerned about ministering with everyone as one army, rather than displaying your gift of dance.

While you are leading aim not to focus on doing movements that match the words of the music, but aim to be keen and flow in what the spirit is doing. Praise and worship is an atmospheric ministry for dance ministers. Although the music may be singing about love and joy, God may be leading the dance ministers to break down strongholds that are hindering the people from receiving true love and joy. If you are lyrics focused you may miss this assignment while doing movements that display the words, yet you are not ministering within the atmosphere and to the people to break them free to receive. Being in tune with the Spirit of God is how your team will be able to shift atmospheres and truly usher in the presence of God, while fulfilling the assignments the Lord may reveal during praise and worship.

When leading, give the dance ministers time to catch on to the movements by ministering them repetitiously rather than changing them. If you recognize that they are not effectively ministering the movement, then change the movement to something simple to get everyone in a place of restored unity. You can also have everyone stop dancing and stand in place until you search out what move to minister. Remember you are not there to entertain, but to minister and give glory to God, while establishing his presence in your midst. So, it is okay to take a moment to regroup if necessary.

- ✓ If you are ministering the words to a song, minister repetitious movements that focus on the major theme of song or what God wants to minister to the people or in the atmosphere at that time.
- ✓ If you are ministering movement of intercession, warfare, decreeing and declaring where you are establishing God's presence, minister repetitious movements in that fashion.
- ✓ If you do minister a sequence of single moves make sure they are simple enough where your team can follow. Minister a verse or sequence of single movements religiously until they catch on and can flow in unison with you.

As you are leading, search out what God desires for the atmosphere and the people. This ensures that your movements are led by the Holy Spirit. Always pray and search out the atmosphere. You can use your prayer language to increase your ability to be able to hear what God is saying and desiring to be ministered. Be open to communicating with everyone on the team what God has revealed to you. He may reveal his will for praise and worship before the service and he also will reveal things continually as you dance.

Be conscious of your team members so you will know if someone else feels led to lead. Be willing to relinquish the lead to your team members. You can always return to the lead if God reveals revelation or movement to you, if what is being ministered is not penetrating the spirit realm, or keeping the team and atmosphere in a place where God's presence is reigning in our midst.

Do not continue to lead if you feel that you are on your last drop of breath. Yes, it is awesome to put %100 into your dance, but if you are tired, be mindful to allow someone to relieve you when you need to take a break. Continuing to dance when you are tired will cause you to rush off, and depending on where you have taken the team in the spirit realm, you may leave the group susceptible to attack if you leave in a rushed manner and break the fortification of the front line. However, do aim to strengthen yourself and gain endurance, but not to the point of exhaustion, or where you feel like you have nothing left.

Encourage the dance minister that is leading. Do not be dancing behind them with a spirit of envy, despondency, negativity, etc. Let them know they are doing well, especially if they are new to leading, and verbally praise and worship God as this empowers the leader. If you feel a movement needs to be changed or if a specific type of dance needs to go forth, tell them that, and give them an opportunity to lead the team in ministering in that fashion. Or if you feel you should be leading at that moment then tell them that, lead the ministry and then when you have finished what God is saying, let that person return to leading.

During times of intense warfare, or when the person leading is needing help to bring in a complete shift, one team member can stand behind the person leading to fortify, empower, and assist them in fully breaking through. The person leading will be pressing in their full ability and their movements will be powerful and effective, but they are just needing some help to breakthrough demonic resistance and walls. The person that steps behind them should be praying for them, while making sure that they are dancing full force and in sync with the movements of the person leading. They can speak in tongues, pray in English, and speak encouragement to the person to empower them to keep going. This strategy is much like Exodus 17 when Aaron and Hur held up Moses' hands because Israel only prevailed in battle against Amalek when his hands were raised. They held his hands up until the sun went down, fortifying him as the Israelites fought to victory over the Amalekites.

> ***Exodus 17:11-13 English Standard Version*** *Whenever Moses held up his hand, Israel prevailed, and whenever he lowered his hand, Amalek prevailed. But Moses' hands grew weary, so they took a stone and put it under him, and he sat on it, while Aaron and Hur held up his hands, one on one side, and the other on the other side. So his hands were steady until the going down of the sun. And Joshua overwhelmed Amalek and his people with the sword.*

Most dancers do not dance with their entire bodies or they dance through locked knees so their movements look stiff and lethargic. This also tires them out more as it cuts off your circulation and ability for oxygen to flow through your entire body. Dance with your entire body. Ask God to deliver you from insecurity, fear, perversion, lust, rejection, etc. Receive deliverance from root issues that would cause you to feel uncomfortable being abandoned and vulnerable in your movements and body language.

Do not rush off after praise and worship. Seek to stay in the moment with God just in case this time with the Lord is not yet complete. This is key for both praise and worship ministry and for choreographed pieces. You want to make sure not to miss anything that God is wanting to release through your ministry. If you miss it or quench it, subsequently the people and atmosphere will also miss it. Sometimes as dance ministers, we need to demonstrate how to receive from the dance piece or praise and worship ministry that just went forth. Or we need to demonstrate how to remain with God and breakthrough to deliverance and healing. Staying in the moment allows for this, and gives the Holy Spirit an opportunity to respond to the ministry that has just been deposited in the people and the atmosphere, and for heaven to enmesh with earth, where miracles, signs and wonders follow. Seek not just to minister, but to see God be demonstrated through what you minister. STAY IN THE MOMENT!

It is important for dance ministers to make sure that you are wearing the appropriate undergarments under your dance clothing. It can be a distraction to both you and the audience if the undergarments are not the correct type, do not fit for your body shape, if they are all types of wild colors, and can be seen through your dance garment. The appearance of the team is also a part of the ministry, as your garments and clothing are a part of your mantle and tell who you are. Aaron and the priests had garments that identified who they were that God specifically designed and ordained for them. It is the same for you as a minister of dance. Your dance garments should fit well and be loose fitting and not snug. People should not be focused on your body parts and figure, but on God. Personal grooming is necessary as this is a ministry that is presented before the people and before God. Even if you do not wear makeup which is perfectly okay, you want to make sure that your face is looking nice and your hair is neat. You are kings and queens ministering before, unto, and for your KING. Come to him with the best of you as he will always be giving you the best of him.

As the Holy Spirit leads, pull the audience up to dance with you and the team. This releases a greater presence of salvation and liberty into the atmosphere, and unveils a greater weighty presence of God. God responds to praise and worship, so the more reverence is released, the more you can discern his presence in your midst.

> ***Psalms 22:3*** *But thou art holy, O thou that inhabitest the praises of Israel.*
> ***Matthew 18:20*** *For where two or three are gathered together in my name, there am I in the midst of them.*

Display eye contact. Use wisdom as when to intentionally:

- ✓ Engage God
- ✓ Engage the audience
- ✓ Engage those you are ministering with
- ✓ Engage the directions of your movements
- ✓ Engage the atmosphere
- ✓ Engage the spirit realm
- ✓ Pierce and fiercely engage the devil and demonic strongholds

BE PRESENT IN YOUR DANCE BY DISPLAYING EYE CONTACT!

> ***Matthew 6:22-23*** *The light of the body is the eye: if therefore thine eye be single, thy whole body shall be full of light. But if thine eye be evil, thy whole body shall be full of darkness. If therefore the light that is in thee be darkness, how great is that darkness!*

Remember you are a demonstration of salvation and liberty to the people and the atmosphere.

The word "*single* "in the Greek is *haplous* and actually means *clear, whole, good fulfilling its office* (fulfilling your office as a licensed dance minister).

- ✓ Your eyes reveal God's governmental authority upon your life to usher people into the Holies of Holies.

- ✓ Your eyes reveal the motive and vision of how God desires to use your body.
- ✓ Your eyes reveal the knowledge and direction of the Lord.
- ✓ Your eyes also reveal the glory of God that is in your body and being released through your body.

If your eyes are displaying shame, guilt, fear, timidity, hesitancy to connect with people and spheres, pride, perversion, need for validation and approval, etc., then this is what will be revealed and released through your movements. This also reveals a level of deliverance is needed in your soul, emotions, and identity.

Darkness is "*scotos*" in the Greek and means, "*shadiness, obscurity, and ignorance with respecting divine things and human duties.*" When somethings is obscure, it is unclear, hard to perceive and understand, vague, ambiguous (subject to different meanings), doubtful, unclear in nature. This is part of what causes people to resist dance ministry. We must make sure we are clear in our identity and calling and are displaying that so people will be clear that dance ministry is of God.

Dance through the fullness of the fruit of the spirit where healthy emotions shine forth.

> ***Galatians 5:22-26*** *But the fruit of the Spirit is love, joy, peace, longsuffering, gentleness, goodness, faith, meekness, temperance: against such there is no law. And they that are Christ's have crucified the flesh with the affections and lusts. If we live in the Spirit, let us also walk in the Spirit. Let us not be desirous of vain glory, provoking one another, envying one another.*

The fruits of the Holy Spirit are, charity, joy, peace, patience, kindness, goodness, generosity, gentleness, faithfulness, modesty, self-control, chastity. Other fruits of the Holy Spirit would be confidence, boldness, strength, power, authority, grace, wellness, wholeness, etc. Spend consistent time asking the Holy Spirit to empower you with his fruit so you will be able to minister and live through God's character, nature, and likeness.

Dance through the thoughts, mind and identity of God. Focus on what pleases God rather than negativity, or fear, the audience, soul issues, etc. As you seek to have the thoughts, mind and identity of God when ministering in dance, you will release his essence to the people and in the atmosphere.

> ***Philippians 4:8 The Amplified Bible*** *Finally, brethren, whatsoever things are true, whatsoever things are honest (honoring, health in character), whatsoever things are just (equitable (fruitful producing), holy, righteous, virtuous, establishing of God's law and order) whatsoever things are pure (clean, chaste, free from carnality), whatsoever things are lovely (friendly, pleasing, acceptable), whatsoever things are of good report (reputable, God's words and will, prophetic, revelatory, speaking audaciously (extremely bold or daring; recklessly brave; fearless); if there be any virtue (the identity of God), and if there be any praise (exaltation of God), think on these things.*

Minister through the sevenfold spirit of God. This will enable you to minister movements that produce God's will in your midst. He will give you revelation of movements he wants you to do and the reason for the movements.

> ***Isaiah 11:2*** *And the spirit of the Lord shall rest upon him, the spirit of wisdom and understanding, the spirit of counsel and might, the spirit of knowledge and of the fear of the Lord.*

Focus on ministering through the Holy Spirit. This also enables you to minister through God's power and strength, while giving you more endurance and stamina as opposed to ministering through your own strength where you tire easily and are zapped by religion, tradition and other demonic spirits.

> ***Zechariah 4:6*** *Then he answered and spake unto me, saying, This is the word of the Lord unto Zerubbabel, saying, Not by might, nor by power, but by my spirit, saith the Lord of hosts.*

Your dance is a gift, but it is not the sum total of who you are. You are called as some type of minister of God who just happen to have the gift of dance. Knowing your calling endues your gifts with the unique identity of God. It also empowers your gift of dance and every other gift you have with the power, authority, and dominion that God has placed on your life.

> ***Luke 4:18*** *The Spirit of the Lord is upon me, because he hath anointed me to preach the gospel to the poor; he hath sent me to heal the brokenhearted, to preach deliverance to the captives, and recovering of sight to the blind, to set at liberty them that are bruised.*

> ***Ephesians 4:11*** *And he gave some, apostles; and some, prophets; and some, evangelists; and some, pastors and teachers. Knowing your calling gives your gifts vision so you know why God uses you, how he uses you and your purpose in the earth realm.*

References

Scripture references are from:

www.biblegateway.com

www.blueletterbible.com

www.crosswalk.com

www.Wikipedia.com

Definitions are quoted from:

www.answers.com

www.m-w.com

www.dictionary.com

Book Cover designed by Reenita Keys.

Connect with her via Facebook.

Kingdom Shifters Books & Apparel

Available at Kingdomshifters.com

BOOKS FOR EVERYONE

Healing The Wounded Leader   Kingdom Shifters Decree That Thang

There Is An App For That   Kingdom Watchman Builder On the Wall

Embodiment Of A Kingdom Watchman
Dismantling Homosexuality Handbook   Releasing The Vision   Feasting In His Presence

Kingdom Heirs Decree That Thing   Let There Be Sight

Atmosphere Changers (Weaponry)   Apostolic Governing

BOOKS FOR DANCERS

Dancers! Dancers! Decree That Thang

Spirits That Attack Dance Ministers & Ministries

TEE SHIRTS

Kingdom Shifters Tee Shirt   Let The Fruit Speak Tee Shirt

Releasing The Vision Tee Shirt   Kingdom Perspective Tee Shirt

Stand in Position Tee Shirt   No Defense Tee Shirt

My God Rules Like A Boss Tee Shirt   Destiny Blueprint Tee Shirt

CD'S

Decree That Thing CD

Kingdom Heirs Decree That Thing CD

Teachings & Worship CD's

www.ingramcontent.com/pod-product-compliance
Lightning Source LLC
LaVergne TN
LVHW020719110826
845149LV00012B/2336

9780999004173